AF880266

THE OFFICIAL

YOUTH SOCCER BOOK

THE OFFICIAL YOUTH SOCCER BOOK of The United States Youth Soccer Association

by Karl-Heinz Schreiber

An Official Publication of the United States Soccer Federation

Rand McNally & Company
Chicago • New York • San Francisco

Acknowledgments

The author wishes to thank his soccer friends from the USYSA for their suggestions after reviewing the manuscript. Special recognition is due the editors at Rand McNally, for their help and patience, and to Lee Wilder Snider, who produced most of the illustrations. Not surprisingly, they all became avid soccer fans.

—K.S.

Library of Congress Cataloging in Publication Data

Schreiber, Karl-Heinz, [date]
The official youth soccer book of the United States Youth Soccer Association.

"An official publication of the United States Soccer Federation."
1. Soccer. 2. Soccer—United States. I. United States Soccer Federation. II. Title.
GV943.S335 1983 796.334'0973 83-11212
ISBN 0-528-88059-4

Picture Credits

Cover photos by Stan Green

Chuck Browne, pages 41, 74
Stan Green, pages 2, 13, 59, 91, 113
Jerry Hite, pages 8, 16, 21, 31, 37, 38, 73, 78, 79, 83, 86, 89, 97, 106
Karl-Heinz Schreiber, pages 70, 103

Drawings in Chapters 1, 2, and 3 by Lee Wilder Snider

© Rand McNally & Company 1983
All rights reserved
Printed in the United States of America
First printing 1983

Contents

Youth Soccer in the United States

During the last two decades, soccer in the United States has experienced boomlike expansion and growth at the youth level. The main reasons for this sudden breakthrough are community-oriented organizations supported by parent volunteers and an emphasis on recreational play to encourage the participation of every child interested in the sport, regardless of ability level. Local youth programs have begun to flourish in many parts of the country under the leadership of soccer associations as well as independent organizations, including boys' clubs, church groups, YMCA chapters, and others.

Although there are many organizations running youth soccer programs throughout the United States, those affiliated with the United States Soccer Federation (USSF) are numerically the strongest. The USSF is the only organization in the United States recognized as the national governing body for soccer by the U.S. Olympic Committee and by international associations.

The USSF administers all areas of soccer, including the professional level, unique for a national sports organization. The USSF basically has three divisions: senior (adult) amateur, youth, and professional, each administering its respective program more or less independently but under the overall guidance of the parent organization. Collegiate and high school athletic associations also maintain a liaison relationship with the USSF.

The USSF promotes soccer in the United States; organizes and administers national and international competition; forms and operates national teams, including the U.S. Olympic team; sets up educational and technical programs, such as coaching schools and systems for referee training and licensing; and assigns administrative, promotional, and developmental tasks to affiliated organizations, state associations, or divisions.

In 1974, the United States Youth Soccer Association (USYSA) was formed as the youth division of the USSF. It is a national organization, with affiliates in all 50 states and the District of Columbia, for the promotion, development, and coordination of soccer programs for youngsters under 19 years of age. The success of this nonprofit volunteer organization is reflected in the statistics. In 1975 there were 103,432 registered players, boys and girls, in the United States Youth Soccer Association; in 1982 there were 938,036. In addition to the USYSA-affiliated state associations and their leagues and clubs, there are a number of independent youth soccer organizations with an estimated 500,000 players.

At the high school level, soccer has been well established for years in many parts of the eastern United States. Now, parallel to the recent development of youth soccer in USYSA programs, soccer has established itself as both an intramural and interscholastic sport in high schools in practically all parts of the country. In 1982, there were 213,036 players competing in high school soccer, 51,869 girls and 161,167 boys. Of 51 state high school athletic associations (including the District of Columbia), 38 sanction varsity soccer for boys and 28 for girls.

The mass-participation emphasis of the vast majority of youth soccer programs under USYSA auspices, and a competitive structure that enables youngsters to participate at their level of ability, make playing soccer fun and give it widespread appeal among youngsters. Another factor contributing to soccer's popularity, and a good reason to join or start a youth program, is that soccer under USYSA rules and guidelines is the safest team contact sport and has the lowest injury rate. Playing soccer is also excellent for developing cardiovascular fitness. And soccer is not an expensive sport; a pair of shorts, a T-shirt, and some sneakers are all a player needs in terms of equipment.

Soccer, although called the universal game for many years because it is played on all continents and in almost every country, did not truly become a universal sport until girls and women began to join soccer clubs and leagues a few years ago. Today soccer has become an established sport for girls.

There are no differences in the playing rules for girls and boys in soccer. It is the policy of the USYSA to develop and organize identical programs for both girls' teams and boys' teams, whenever and wherever that is possible. Many USYSA state associations have reached a numerical level of participation that allows separate programs for boys' and girls' teams, and equal programs for both are provided. In the early phase of a youth program combined, or "mixed," teams are appropriate. Experience has shown, however, that once there are enough players, the separate-but-equal concept is most conducive to the overall development of the individuals participating in the sport.

The spectrum of youth soccer reaches from supervised sandlot games to neighborhood and intercity leagues, and includes a wide variety of invitational tournaments all over the country, sociocultural exchanges, and state, regional, and national championships.

Opportunities for youth competition are also available on the international level. The sport and the Laws of the Game (rules of play) are uniform throughout the world, with all national associations (including the USSF) governed by one central body, the Fédération Internationale de Football Association (FIFA), known in English as the International Federation of Association Football. Headquartered in Zurich, Switzerland, FIFA organizes the world's largest international team sports competition, the World Cup, in which a world soccer champion is crowned once every four years. The Olympic soccer competition, which in concept follows the format of the World Cup, also takes place under the auspices of FIFA.

In 1977 FIFA introduced the World Youth Tournament under the cosponsorship of The Coca-Cola Company. This international competition for Under-19 national teams holds finals every two years. In addition, FIFA is currently planning the World Tournament for Schoolboys, for youngsters up to 16 years of age.

Affiliation with FIFA opens the doors for our youth teams to take part in tournaments and sociocultural exchanges with foreign teams and to invite players and teams from other countries to visit us. Hundreds of U.S. teams of all age divisions and levels of competitiveness exchange with teams from Canada and Mexico each year. An ever-increasing number seek the adventure of exploring new territories and making friends on other continents by traveling overseas.

The Official Youth Soccer Book introduces newcomers of all ages to the world of soccer. It was written for young children and for teenagers, for those who have never kicked a soccer ball and those who are experienced players. It was written for grown-ups, too—for parents who are curious to know more about the game their children are involved in, as well as for adults who participate in a local soccer program as volunteers, coaches, officials, or administrators.

The basic elements of the game—playing rules, fundamental skills, and principles of teamwork—are explained in simple terms as an introduction to the sport for novice players and a valuable reference for players who are members of a club or league. A chapter on backyard soccer offers many useful hints and ideas for enjoyable activities players can try on their own, with a few friends, or with members of their family.

Special attention is given in these pages to the needs of players in the youngest age groups. Complete USYSA recommendations for adapting rules of play and field dimensions for very young athletes are provided, along with general suggestions for the coaching and training program.

The final chapters outline "organized soccer" as it operates under USYSA auspices. Detailed descriptions of the functions of a local soccer organization should be helpful to adults active in youth soccer and particularly valuable to those who want to start a community program.

If you are not already a player, coach, parent volunteer, official, or administrator, *The Official Youth Soccer Book* is both an invitation and a guide to becoming involved in the universal game. You are sure to enjoy it.

Chapter 1

Soccer in Brief

The classical game of soccer, known in countries outside the United States and Canada as football or association football, was developed to its present form in Great Britain. In North America the sport eventually was called soccer (a British slang expression from "assoc," the common abbreviation for association football) to distinguish it from the other game of football, the one played with an oval ball, which emerged as a popular sport in the United States and Canada.

Today soccer is the most popular team sport in the world, often called the universal game because of its tremendous following in Europe, Asia, Africa, Australia, South America, and now North America. It is also perhaps the world's oldest team sport. While the development of modern soccer is attributed to the British, the game's origins can be traced back almost 5,000 years.

Sometime around 3000 BC a soccerlike game was played by soldiers in China. Each team had a captain, and players were assigned specific positions. The ball consisted of a leather skin stuffed with animal hair. It was about 1,000 years later that people learned how to make balls filled with air, the most common being the inflated bladder of an animal.

From China this game, called *tsu chu,* was imported to Japan, where it was developed into a religious game called *kemari.*

About 2000 BC soccerlike games were also played in the area around the Mediterranean Sea. The Greeks named their game *episkyros,* and the Romans called theirs *harpastum.* Some historians assume that the Roman legions brought *harpastum* to the British Isles, where eventually it was integrated into the games the inhabitants played at the time, and the result was a sort of rugby-soccer.

This game became quite popular in the Middle Ages. At approximately the time of the legendary Robin Hood, the game was played between village teams, often consisting of a hundred players each, who frequently kicked at things other than the ball—such as opposing players. The matches (also called "mellays," from which the term "melee" was derived) often deteriorated into fierce fights, and rugby-soccer repeatedly was forbidden by ruling kings desiring to maintain law and order.

Besides England, France and Italy were also early "soccer powers" in Europe, competing avidly at about the time Columbus sailed to discover America. In the middle of the 19th century, the rugby-soccer of the Middle Ages began to develop on two separate tracks, and the result was two distinct sports—soccer as we know it today and rugby. The sport of rugby is still popular in England, France, and other countries. But it is played with an oval ball and has many other similarities to American football, which many believe evolved from rugby.

In 1863 the first soccer organization was founded, known as the English Football Association. Today the international governing body for the sport of soccer is FIFA, the Fédération Internationale de Football Association. Founded in 1904 by seven national soccer associations, FIFA has become a kind of "United Nations of Soccer," with more than 150 affiliated national associations divided among six continental federations. The United States, Canada, and Mexico belong to the Confederation of North and Central American and Caribbean Soccer Associations.

FIFA's principal functions are to sanction national governing organizations, such as the United States Soccer Federation; organize and administer international developmental programs; assure compliance with FIFA rules by all national organizations and their affiliates; supervise international competition and player transfers; and organize international competition events, such as the World Cup.

The United States Soccer Federation (USSF) was formed in 1913, under the original name of United States Soccer Football Association. Soccer made some progress in a few metropolitan areas, mostly among ethnic neighborhood groups, but it did not become a national sport in the United States as it had elsewhere. Still, the United States was successful in early World Cup competitions. In 1930 the U.S. national team advanced to the semifinals before falling to Yugoslavia. Four years later the U.S. team reached the final playoffs but was eliminated by Italy. A most impressive triumph for the United States was the 1–0 victory over a star-studded English team in the preliminary round of the 1950 World Cup finals in Brazil, a major upset that sent England home and shocked the international soccer world. In the United States, however, hardly anyone took notice. Since that time the U.S. national team has not been able to qualify for the World Cup final rounds through the zone playoff system, which requires them first to eliminate Mexico and Canada, then defeat the best teams from Central America and the Caribbean countries.

In the United States and Canada, local professional and semiprofessional leagues did not attract sizable crowds in the past, although the sport has had a loyal following. In fact, the oldest professional league in the United States, the American Soccer League, has been in existence for more than 50 years. National championships for professional and semiprofessional teams began in 1914 and for senior amateur teams in 1923. The first national youth championship tournament dates back to 1935. The formation in 1967 of two national

professional leagues, with teams composed almost entirely of foreign players, ended in financial disaster. The fragments of both leagues were merged in 1968 to form the North American Soccer League (NASL). The NASL has generally enjoyed steady progress, with increasing attendance figures and broader exposure on television. The NASL creates professional opportunities for highly talented U.S. and Canadian players who "graduate" from youth soccer programs or college soccer and generates increased interest in the sport among the general public, the business world, and community administrations.

A popular variation of the game today is indoor soccer, which has become a seasonal alternative during the winter months in some parts of the United States and Canada. Indoor soccer was recently introduced at the professional level by the Major Indoor Soccer League (MISL) and has so far been successful. The field for this game corresponds to the size of an ice-hockey rink, and team size is reduced from 11 to six players. Youth and adult amateur teams often use school gymnasiums for their indoor soccer programs.

A Ball, a Field, and Two Goals

Soccer requires a bare minimum of equipment and can be played on any piece of open ground that is relatively level. The schoolyard, a playground, the beach, a street (if there is no traffic)—almost any unobstructed area will do for a pickup game. A couple of spare balls and some plastic cups, coats, or other objects that can be used to mark the goals are all that is needed for an informal game.

Requirements for a formal match are more stringent but even so are relatively simple: The ball should be one designed for soccer, the official ball being 27 to 28 inches in circumference and weighing 14 to 16 ounces. The field of play should be at least 100 yards long and 50 yards wide. At each end is a goal, consisting of two goalposts eight yards apart and connected with a crossbar eight feet above the ground. (For younger players the USYSA advocates scaled-down dimensions for both the ball and the field of play. These and other game modifications recommended for youth players will be covered in detail in this and subsequent chapters.)

Another aspect of soccer's simplicity is the game itself. There are basically just two elements: defending one's goal and trying to propel the ball into the other team's goal. Moving the ball is accomplished primarily by kicking, either passing it or dribbling it. If the ball goes into a team's goal, a "goal" is scored by the opposition. The team having scored the most goals at the end of the game is the winner.

Although soccer is simple in concept, it is neither slow nor routine. To the contrary, from the moment of the opening kickoff it is a game of almost constant action. There are no time-outs, and the flow of play is interrupted only briefly when a ball goes out-of-bounds, a free kick is called, a goal scored, or a player injured. Action is continuous as players switch from offense to defense, time and again. The pattern of the game, ever changing, is determined solely by the play on the field.

In order to make the game uniform throughout the world as well as to protect players from injuries, there is a set of rules—called the Laws of the Game—defined by FIFA and adhered to by national associations worldwide, including the USSF. Modifications for youth soccer, such as team size, time of play, and size and weight of the ball, can be approved by a national body. The references in this book, unless otherwise specified, are to the official "international" rules. A summary of the Laws of the Game, as well as approved modifications for youth soccer, may be found in the Appendix.

Number of Players and Their Equipment

A soccer team consists of 11 players: one goalkeeper and ten field players. The basic field positions are forwards (also known as strikers or wingers), midfielders (also known as halfbacks or linkmen), and defenders (also known as fullbacks or backs). In today's soccer, however, field players often switch positions during play, so they are not necessarily defined as playing a particular position. For example, because of the flow of play or a given situation, a fullback might suddenly switch to the position of a midfielder or wing.

The USYSA organizes youth play into six age divisions: Under 19, Under 16, Under 14, Under 12, Under 10, and Under 8. These age divisions comprise players who are under the age specified before the first day of January during the playing season. It is a policy that a player who has the needed physical and technical ability may "play up," that is, a 13-year-old boy or girl could play on an Under-16 team. But an older player may never "play down"—a 13-year-old could not play on an Under-12 team, for example.

Under USYSA rules, there can be up to 18 players on a team roster. In a game this means there could be as many as seven players on the sideline. It is USYSA policy that each player on a team be given the opportunity to play part of every game, as long as the player has attended practices regularly and otherwise adheres to team, club, or league rules. In order to assure players of as much game time as possible, coaches and administrators should strive to keep team rosters as small as is practicable.

For children 10 years of age or under, the USYSA recommends mini-soccer games, with a reduced number of players on a side; for example, nine players for teams of 9- and 10-year-olds, seven players for teams of 8-year-olds.

One player is appointed team captain by the coach. The captain should demonstrate leadership and sportsmanship and provide encouragement to his teammates. During the game he may assist the coach by relaying tactical instructions to the players on the field. Soccer etiquette requires that before a game starts, the captain introduce himself to the referee and the other team captain, shake hands with them, and give the name of his team and club.

The proper uniform for a player consists of a jersey or shirt, shorts, socks, and soccer shoes. The goalkeeper must wear a jersey or sweater that is different in color from those of both his team and the opposing team. Shin guards, although not required, are recommended for all players, to protect the lower leg above the ankle. Soccer is played in any weather, rain or shine, sometimes even on snow, if the field can be properly prepared. On cool days an extra shirt may be worn beneath the jersey. Because there is continuous running action, there is normally no need for extra clothing such as stocking hats, long pants, coats, or gloves, even on relatively cold days. A player should, however, bring a coat, sweater, perhaps sweat pants or a warm-up suit, so that he or she can keep warm while not playing.

One important aspect of the Laws of the Game deals with the safety of equipment and the playing field, geared to avoid injuries among

players. It is the responsibility of the referee before the start of the game to inspect the field, including the goals, and make sure that any potentially dangerous objects are removed or unsafe conditions corrected. Another of the referee's duties is to inspect the players' uniforms and shoes to ensure that items that might be hazardous are removed, such as certain zippers, hats or caps, wristwatches, rings—anything that could hurt another player who came in contact with it.

A large assortment of special soccer shoes is now available. You can generally assume that they will comply with the regulations specified in the official rules. However, in the case of multipurpose shoes, it is advisable to check the size and the design of the cleats. FIFA rules specify in detail the size of the stud on the sole of a soccer shoe: The round studs must be cylindrical or conical in shape and nowhere less than ½ inch thick; they must not be more than ¾ inch high. They can be made of rubber, leather, plastic, or aluminum. On shoes with replaceable studs, the screw must be part of the stud, *not* the sole of the shoe. Nowadays, most soccer shoes have studs that are molded as part of the sole. If there are at least ten studs per sole they are permitted, provided their minimum diameter is at least ⅜ inch.

Ordinary gym shoes or sneakers can also be worn, especially in low-pressure recreational programs or for the younger age groups. Coaches, referees, or other responsible adults should see to it that all players show up with the same type of footwear. A player wearing studded shoes can easily hurt another player wearing sneakers if he accidentally steps on his foot.

Each boy and girl should have a soccer ball for the chief purpose of individual practice. Soccer balls are available in many different materials and price ranges. For general practice at home or on the playground, an inexpensive fiber-reinforced plastic ball will serve quite well.

The Field of Play

Although soccer can be played in practically any area that is both large enough and free of obstructions, the Laws of the Game specify the dimensions and field markings required for an official match. These are shown in the accompanying diagram.

The best surface for a game is grass, but a well-prepared dirt field can also be used. It is important, however, that no large rocks or other potentially dangerous objects be on the field of play.

The dimensions shown in the diagram are for older youth and adult games. The width and length of the field can vary considerably. The field size recommended by FIFA for international matches is 70 to 80 yards wide and 110 to 120 yards long. The other dimensions, such as the penalty area and the center circle, are standard. For very young players modifications are recommended, with field size, goal size, and other dimensions scaled down, as detailed in Chapter 5. Dimensions may also be scaled down for indoor soccer matches.

The halfway line divides the field into two equal sections. The lateral boundaries are referred to as touchlines or sidelines. The end lines are called goal lines. At the four corners, there are corner flags on posts extending at least five feet above the ground. The tops of the posts must be rounded off. The quarter circle at each corner defines the area in which the ball is placed for a corner kick, which is taken by the attacking team when a defender kicks the ball over his own goal line. When an attacker kicks the ball over the goal line, however, the defending team restarts the match with a goal kick taken from within the goal area, or more precisely, from the half of the goal area nearest the place where the ball was kicked out. The goal area also provides some protection for the goalkeeper, because a field player is not allowed to make body contact with the goalkeeper in that area.

The larger rectangular area in front of the goal is called the penalty area. In the event a defender commits any of the nine direct-kick offenses in this area (see "Fair or Foul" later on in this chapter), the attacking team is awarded a penalty kick, taken from the penalty mark. It is a one-on-one situation, and only the goalkeeper, standing on the goal line in the middle of the goal, and the player taking the kick are allowed inside the penalty area. All the other players must be at least ten yards from the ball; the penalty arc marks the ten-yard area from which the players are excluded.

Another rule regarding the penalty area concerns the goalkeeper. This is the only area in which he is allowed to play the ball with his hands. Outside the penalty area, goalkeepers must adhere to the same rules as field players.

Coaches and substitutes should remain in an area near the halfway line and at least three yards behind the touchline. Spectators should also remain three yards behind the touchline. Some fields are marked with a "spectator line." A "photographer's line" is required for games covered by the media, and photographers and other members of the media are restricted to the area behind this line, which is generally a few yards behind the goal line.

Time of Play

A soccer match is divided into two halves of equal length. At halftime, there is at least a five-minute intermission after which the teams

THE FIELD OF PLAY

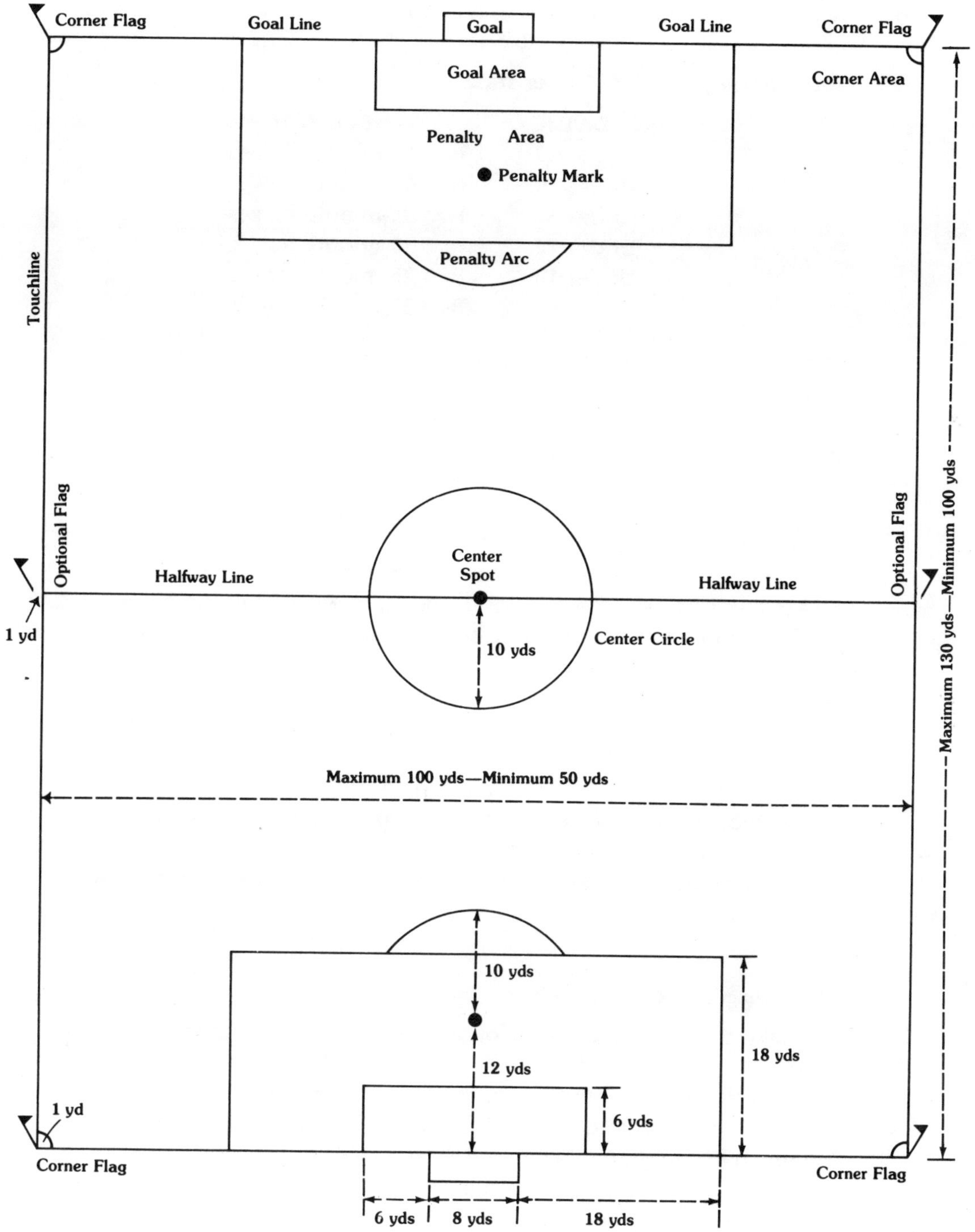

change sides, that is, defend the opposite goal. The total regular playing time is 90 minutes (two 45-minute halves). This makes for a very strenuous workout because the action is sustained and is not interrupted by time-outs. The playing periods have been shortened for younger players. USYSA rules state:

AGE DIVISION	GAME LENGTH
Under 19	Two 45-minute halves
Under 16	Two 40-minute halves
Under 14	Two 35-minute halves
Under 12	Two 30-minute halves
Under 10	Two 25-minute halves
Under 8	Two 25-minute halves

These playing periods are binding for competitions held under the auspices of the USYSA. With USYSA permission, however, state associations may introduce variations, including one-year-increment age divisions, for intrastate play.

Substitutions

The number of substitutions is limited to two per match according to FIFA's Laws of the Game. For youth soccer, however, this has been lifted to allow unlimited substitutions so that each player can have an appreciable amount of playing time. Substitutions are permitted only with the referee's consent. (The referee may decide against a substitution so as not to interrupt the flow of the game.) Substitutions are allowed only at the following times:

- Prior to a throw-in (by team substituting)
- Prior to a goal kick (by either team)
- After a goal (by either team)
- After an injury (either team) when play is stopped by the referee
- At halftime

Referee and Linesmen

To make certain every player follows the rules of the game, a referee is assigned to supervise the action on the field. The referee is assisted by two linesmen, one patrolling each of the touchlines.

The referee's main duty is to ensure that the game is played fairly. When, in his opinion, players violate the rules, the referee will stop play, usually by blowing a whistle. He will then indicate in words or by a signal the decision or penalty. In younger age divisions, the referee will often give a brief explanation as to why the game was stopped, so that players can learn from their mistakes. The referee is the only person who can make calls on infractions of the rules. His decisions must be respected by each player and, of course, by the coaches and spectators.

The referee is also the official timekeeper on the field. But players should refrain from asking him how much time remains—a very common situation among younger players—and instead ask their coach if they feel the need to know.

The two linesmen assist the referee by signaling when a ball goes out of play, if a player is offside, or if they observe any other rule infraction that the referee may have missed. Their duty, however, is merely to inform the referee, who then makes the official determination.

The linesmen are always positioned *outside* the boundaries of the playing field. The referee is always *on* the field of play. It is important to understand that the referee is considered part of the field of play, which means the game continues when the ball hits the referee. If a ball bounces off the referee and into a goal, it is a score.

Start of the Match

The team winning the coin toss has the choice of selecting the goal it wants to defend or of taking the kickoff. (Unlike American football, in

soccer the team kicking off normally retains possession of the ball.) The kickoff is made with a placekick at the center spot. All players must be in their own half of the field and members of the defending team must be at least ten yards from the ball, outside the center circle, until it is in play. The ball must be played forward, and it must travel approximately two feet (or precisely a distance amounting to its circumference) before it can be touched by another player. Note: The player who kicks off cannot touch the ball again until it has been played by another player.

The procedure described above also applies to restarts from a dead ball during the course of a match. In these situations too, opposing players must be ten yards from the ball and the ball must travel two feet before it can be touched by another player. The player restarting the game with a kick cannot touch the ball again before it is played by another player.

Ball In and Out of Play

The most common situation to stop play, especially in games involving younger soccer players, is the out-of-bounds ball. For newcomers to soccer, it is important to remember that the touchlines (sidelines) and goal lines are part of the field of play. Thus, the ball is out of play only when it has *completely passed over* the touchline or goal line. Similarly for scoring, the ball must *completely cross* the goal line, between the goalposts and below the crossbar—the entire projected area of the ball must pass the outer limit of the goal line.

Players and spectators often call for "out" if the center of the ball is outside the line, but as long as the tiniest portion of the ball is still on the line, the ball is in play.

When a ball has gone out of play by crossing over the touchline, it is brought back into play by a throw-in at the spot where it went out-of-bounds. The throw-in is the only time that a field player is permitted to use his hands to propel the ball. It is a special skill and should be practiced regularly. Needless to say, long-distance throw-ins with high accuracy can be an enormous advantage for a team.

The rules are quite specific about the way the throw-in is to be executed. The ball must be delivered from behind the head and must be thrown with *both* hands. Both feet, or at least part of both, must be on the ground, on or outside the touchline, while throwing. If the player violates any of the throw-in rules, the ball is given over to the opposing team for a throw-in. As with a kickoff or a free kick, the player who makes the throw-in is not allowed to play the ball until another player has touched it.

If the ball goes out-of-bounds over a goal line instead of a sideline

Ball In and Out of Play

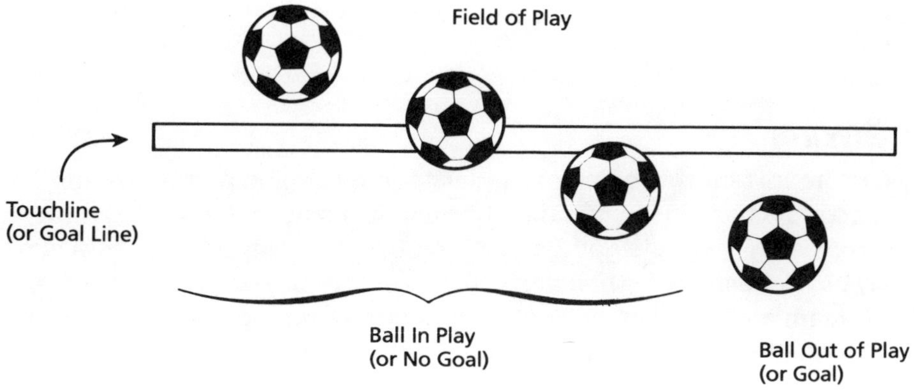

The touchlines and goal lines are part of the field of play, and the ball is not out of play until it has completely passed over these boundary lines. The ball remains in play as long as any portion of it is on the line.

Throw-In

The ball must be thrown with both hands from behind the player's head; part of both feet must be on the ground. A powerful (long-distance) throw-in is achieved by bending the upper body back as far as possible with knees bent, then swinging forward.

and was last touched by the attacking team, the defending team is awarded a goal kick, which is a placekick taken from within the goal area. If the ball is propelled over the goal line by a defender, an attacking player puts the ball back in play with a corner kick (from within the corner arc).

Offside

One important rule often misunderstood by beginning players and spectators pertains to offside. Although it is one of the shortest laws, it covers many possible game situations. Briefly, a player is offside when (1) he is ahead of the ball *at the moment it is played by a member of his team* and (2) there are not at least two opposing players (this can include the goalie) between himself and the other team's goal line. That is the basic rule, but there are exceptions. For example, the rule does not apply in the team's own half of the field. It does not apply if the ball comes from a defending player. Nor does it apply if one's teammate gets the ball directly from a throw-in, a corner kick, a drop ball, or a goal kick.

Another exception to note is the situation in which a player is in an offside position but does not interfere with the game action nor does he try to gain any advantage by being offside. In such a case the game continues, and no penalty is invoked. This is a judgment call by the referee.

Offside: At the moment the ball was kicked, the player receiving the pass had only one opponent (the goalkeeper) between himself and the goal line.

Offside: The player to whom the ball is being kicked has only one player (the goalkeeper) between himself and the goal line and therefore is offside.

Fair or Foul

One of the main purposes of the Laws of the Game is to protect players from injury. This section describes and illustrates some of the violations that can occur during a match.

There are two types of fouls: *Intentionally* rough, unfair, or dangerous play; and behavior that is *unintentionally* unsportsmanlike or dangerous.

The penalty for the first type of offense (intentional) is a *direct* free kick, which the referee signals by pointing with one arm toward the goal of the offending team and with the other arm to the point of the infraction, where the kick is to be taken. Opposing players must remain ten yards from the ball until it is in play. A goal can be scored from a direct free kick; that is, the player taking the kick can kick the ball into the goal without another player having to touch it. There are nine direct free kick offenses:

- Intentionally playing the ball with the hands (includes arms from the shoulders down)
- Intentionally charging an opponent violently or dangerously (ordinary charging—shoulder-to-shoulder contact without arm or elbow action—is not a violation)
- Intentionally charging an opponent from behind

Area covered by "hands"—includes arms from the shoulders down.

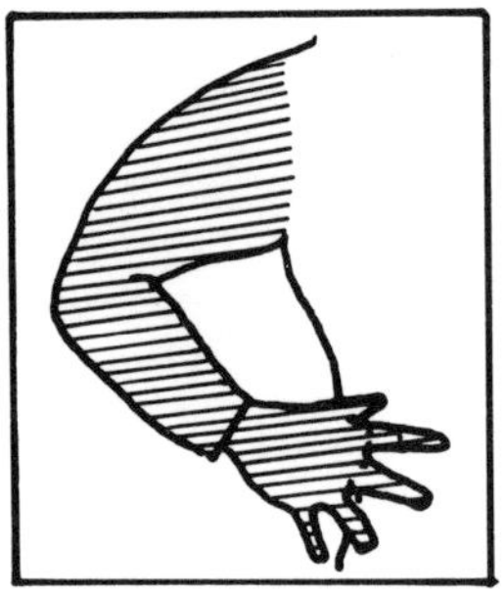

Charging: This is a fair charge; the ball is within playing distance, and the players are leaning against each other with the upper shoulder only.

- Intentionally holding an opponent
- Intentionally pushing an opponent
- Intentionally striking or attempting to strike an opponent
- Intentionally kicking or attempting to kick an opponent
- Intentionally tripping an opponent
- Intentionally jumping at an opponent

If a direct free kick violation is committed by the defenders within their penalty area, the attacking team is awarded a penalty kick, which is taken from the penalty mark with only the goalkeeper to defend against it.

For all other fouls and misconduct, an *indirect* free kick is awarded to the opposing team by the referee, who signals it by raising one arm. As the word "indirect" implies, a goal cannot be scored directly from this type of free kick; the ball must first be touched or played by another player. Offenses for which an indirect free kick is awarded include:

- Playing in a dangerous manner (example: high kick)
- Charging fairly but with the ball not in playing distance
- Obstructing an opponent without playing the ball
- Charging the goalkeeper *except* when (1) he is holding the ball, (2) he is obstructing an opponent, or (3) he is outside the goal area
- When playing as goalie, the player (1) takes more than four steps with the ball without completely releasing it so that it can be played by another, or (2) holds the ball in order to "waste time" and give an unfair advantage to his own team

In order to keep the game moving as much as possible, it is within the referee's discretionary power to refrain from stopping play for infractions if in his judgment this would give an advantage to the offending player or his team. The referee usually indicates by word or hand signal when he applies the "advantage clause."

For persistent infringements of the Laws of the Game, for dissent from the referee's decisions by word or action, or for ungentlemanly conduct, a player will receive a caution. This is a verbal warning from the referee and puts the player on notice that a repeat offense will result in ejection from the match.

In addition to persistent misconduct after having received a caution, more serious offenses such as violent conduct, serious foul play, and foul language will also be penalized by ejection. Since an ejected player cannot be replaced, this is a severe penalty.

It has become standard practice for the referee to signal a caution by showing the player (and the spectators) a yellow card and to signal an ejection by showing a red card. These penalties can also be applied against coaches, assistant coaches, and substitute players at the sidelines.

Fair or Foul—Some Examples

Charge is fair, but ball not within playing distance. Indirect free kick.

Unintentional hand ball. Player at left kicks ball against arm of opponent. No infraction. Play continues.

Fair or Foul—Some Examples

Intentional tripping. Direct free kick.

Holding. Direct free kick.

Unintentional tripping. Player at left has played ball cleanly; opponent arrives late to gain possession and falls over outstretched leg. Play continues.

Pushing—use of elbow. Direct free kick.

Fair or Foul—Some Examples

Player in possession turning to shield ball from opponent. Fair play.

Dangerous play. Indirect free kick.

Obstruction. Player having made a pass to a teammate intentionally obstructs an opponent to prevent her from tackling player receiving ball. Indirect free kick.

Chapter **2**

Basic Soccer Skills

Any youngster who has ever idly kicked an empty pop can, a rock, a tennis ball, or other object would probably enjoy soccer. It is much easier to kick a soccer ball in the desired direction, and the initial frustrations about this seemingly unusual way of propelling a large ball soon disappear with coaching and practice.

Soccer is a game that boys and girls are able to enjoy very quickly, even if they have never played it before. The rules of the game are simple. There are no special requirements in regard to a player's physical size or weight. At the beginner level, one only needs to be reasonably coordinated, and that's basically it. There is, however, one important prerequisite, and that is a fundamental respect for other players, both teammates and opponents. Kicking is always directed at the *ball,* and more than anything else a young player must develop the ability to hit the *ball* and avoid kicking the feet or legs of fellow players.

Some youngsters grow up in areas where soccer is an established sport and may have kicked their first soccer ball shortly after they started to walk. It is even likely some have played soccer with their parents before they were old enough to go to school or perhaps have already participated in an organized soccer program geared specifically toward younger players. They will have a head start. But it is never too late to join a soccer program. The boy or girl who moves to an area where soccer is an established sport will find that it is always possible to

join a team, even if he or she has never played actively before. Most programs operated under USYSA auspices cater to all skill and interest levels, from recreational beginners to the highly competitive. This helps to make soccer fun for the great majority of players and their parents.

It has been stated before that the objective in soccer is to put the ball into the opponent's goal. Propelling the ball can be accomplished with every part of the body except the arms and the hands. The various techniques for doing this are taught during team practices. The following sections here will familiarize the beginning player with the skills that are the fundamental tools of a player. Learning and perfecting them enable the player to master the ball in any situation, and make it possible to play as part of a team by controlling a pass received from a teammate, passing to another player, or shooting at the goal. Improving individual skills is not only important in order to strengthen one's own team, it is also a prerequisite for enjoying the game.

Passing

Perhaps the most basic skill in the game of soccer is passing the ball, that is, the technique of propelling it to a teammate or into an open area, where it can be safely collected by a teammate. Passing is the key to teamwork, which is so essential to soccer.

There are several different ways to push or propel the ball with the feet, among them the inside-of-the-foot pass, outside-of-the-foot pass, instep pass, and chip pass. We will treat only the most basic passes in this section, but a player will eventually learn all forms as he or she progresses in soccer development.

The most common pass is the *inside-of-the-foot pass,* one of the most accurate and easiest to learn. The ball is pushed with the inner side of the foot. But the other foot, the nonkicking one, is also important. It must be positioned properly, alongside the ball with the toe pointing in the direction you want the pass to go.

Move the kicking leg back, with the toe of the kicking foot pointing out and up, and the ankle locked stiff. Swing the leg at the ball—like a golf putter. Keep your upper body over the ball and your eyes on the ball when you hit it. Contact should be made with the inner side of the foot, halfway between the toe and the heel. After hitting the ball, keep your foot in the same position (toe pointing out and up, ankle locked) and continue the leg movement in the direction of the pass.

At first, practice the inside-of-the-foot pass with the ball dead (still). Then try it with a slowly rolling ball, gradually improving your timing at increased speed. You will find that the large area of the side of your foot, as opposed to the small area of your toes, provides good control

Inside-of-the-Foot Pass

Position nonkicking foot alongside ball, toe pointing in direction of intended pass. Swing kicking leg back, toe pointing out and up, ankle locked.

Swing kicking leg at ball, keeping upper body over ball and eyes on ball.

Strike the center of the ball with inner side of foot between toe and heel, leg following through in direction of pass.

for accurate passing. Remember that even though a player is predominantly right-footed or left-footed, he or she should have basic proficiency with the "other" foot. So for this and other passes, be sure to include plenty of practice with both the right and left foot.

Another basic pass is the *outside-of-the-foot pass.* The action is similar to that for the inside-of-the-foot kick, except that the toe of the kicking foot is turned inward and down, and contact with the ball is made with the outer side of the foot.

When you have mastered these basic passing techniques, you can go on to other varieties, such as the instep pass, chip pass, volley and half-volley pass, and heel pass.

Collecting the Ball

When a teammate is passing the ball to you or you are intercepting a pass from a player on the opposing team, you can sometimes play the ball "direct," that is, touch the ball only once to pass it to another player or shoot at goal. However, this is often not possible or at least rather difficult, and so you have to bring the ball under control first.

The ball can be collected or trapped on the ground with the foot, or in the air with the foot, thigh, chest, or even the head. In game action

Outside-of-the-Foot Pass

Position nonkicking foot alongside ball, toe pointing in direction of intended pass. Swing leg back, toe pointing down and in, ankle locked.

Swing kicking leg at ball, keeping upper body over ball and eyes on ball.

Strike the center of the ball with outer side of foot, leg following through in direction of pass.

it is important to run toward the approaching·ball and at the moment of impact relax and withdraw the "catching" surface of the body, providing a cushion effect to slow the ball down. When you collect a ball in the air, bring it to the ground quickly and immediately play it by passing on to another player or shooting at goal.

Collecting Low Balls with the Inside of the Foot

Move the leg forward to meet the ball with the inner side of the foot.

Immediately as contact is made, move the leg back to cushion the impact and slow the ball down.

Bring the ball far back to control it and stop it dead.

Collecting High Balls with the Chest

Arch your body backward to meet the ball with the center of the chest.
Bend the knees to aid in cushioning the ball.

Straighten your body immediately as contact is made so that the ball drops directly to the ground.

Collecting High Balls with the Thigh

Meet the ball in midair with the thigh, letting ball land midway between the knee and the top of the thigh.

As contact is made, withdraw the thigh so that the ball drops to the ground.

Collecting High Balls with the Instep

Meet the ball in midair with the instep.

Immediately as contact is made, pull the foot with the ball to the ground.

Collecting High Balls with the Inside of the Foot

Move the raised leg to meet the ball with the inner side of the foot.

As contact is made, pull the leg back to cushion the impact and let the ball drop to the ground.

Shooting

Shooting is another important skill that young players will need to master. The basic technique for shooting is the *instep kick.* Note: You do *not* use the toe, except perhaps in desperate situations, such as when you cannot reach a fast-approaching ball and swing your foot at it properly. The small area of impact when shooting with the toe gives you less control.

The instep is the upper surface of the arch of the foot, between the ankle and the toes. That is the area of the foot you use to propel the ball for an instep kick. Proper lacing of the shoes is important, and that becomes apparent with the instep kick. If you lace your shoes in the usual way and tie the bow on the top of your foot, it might hurt when you kick with the instep. Therefore, shoelaces should be long enough to wrap around the foot, and the bow should be tied on the outer side of your foot. Then the laces will not get in the way when you instep kick.

The action of shooting is similar to that of passing. You position the nonkicking foot alongside the ball. Then swing the kicking foot at the ball, but with the toe pointing downward and the ankle locked. Strike the ball with the instep. Your leg should follow through in the direction of the shot, just as in passing.

Shooting with the Instep

Run toward ball and plant nonkicking foot alongside, toe pointing in intended direction of shot. Kicking leg should be raised, with toe pointing down and ankle locked.

Swing kicking leg through the ball, instep striking center of ball.

Kicking leg follows through in direction of shot.

Proper lacing of the shoes requires shoelaces that are long enough to wrap around the foot so that the bow can be tied on the outer side of the foot rather than on top.

After gradually building up confidence with this technique, try to improve accuracy and power. Although the goal seems enormous to the goalkeeper defending it, it is very small from the perspective of a player attacking it. Plenty of practice will help you direct your shots consistently on target.

A special word of advice: Even more in shooting than in passing, the positioning of the nonkicking foot is of essential importance. If you place the toe of the nonkicking foot behind the center of the ball, the shot will most likely go high in the air and over the crossbar.

Most players develop a preference for shooting with one specific foot, becoming left-footed or right-footed players. This kind of specialization is natural, but a player who can shoot well with either foot certainly has an advantage under game pressure. So your practice should include shooting with the right and the left foot.

As you become more experienced, you will move on to other shooting techniques, such as the half-volley drive, the volley, or the overhead-volley kick. But first you should master the basic instep shot.

Heading

To the novice soccer player or spectator, the technique of heading is one of the most unusual ways to propel a ball. This skill is used for either passing or shooting on goal when there is not enough time to collect a high ball in the air and get it to the ground to pass or shoot.

In order to avoid injury, it is important to execute this skill correctly. The ball is hit with the center of the *forehead*—never the upper portion of the head. Keep your chin down and neck stiff, and use the swing of your upper body to generate force. Keep your mouth shut but your

Contact Area in Heading

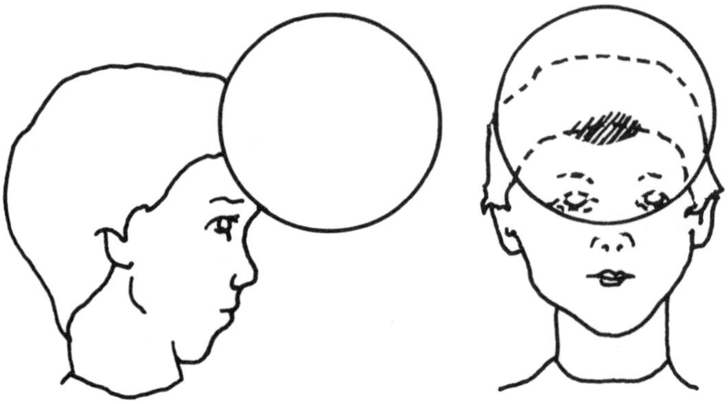

Tuck the chin into the chest and keep your eyes open until the moment of impact.

Hit the ball with the upper forehead at the hairline.

Heading the Ball

Prepare to meet the ball with feet spread and knees flexed, arching your back from the hips.

Keeping your eyes on the ball, tuck your chin into your chest and swing your upper body forward, striking the ball with the upper forehead.

As contact is made, release the chin, following through with the forehead.

eyes open—at least until you make contact with the ball.

In the beginning, you may want to practice heading with a light ball. Using a round, air-filled balloon makes it possible to practice heading in "slow motion" and is a good way to start developing proficiency. It is fun and can be done just about anywhere, even in your room. When you are familiar with the technique, you can use a regular soccer ball with much more confidence.

Coaches generally emphasize a very careful approach to heading, particularly with players under 10 years old, and as an alternative usually stress collecting high balls with the chest or thigh and bringing them to the ground quickly.

As in other skills, timing is the basis for a successful header, be it a shot on goal or a pass to a teammate. Don't wait for the ball to come to you. Go to meet it! A player from the other team will also be trying to play the ball, so you must jump to meet the ball *first*.

Dribbling

Although success in soccer is keyed to good teamwork, there are many situations in which a player has to rely solely on individual skills. One of these skills is dribbling, that is, controlling the ball while moving it past one or more opponents by a series of soft touches with the foot. The dribbler makes changes in pace and direction in order to "fake out" opposing players (a technique called feinting).

In learning to dribble, first use short inside-of-the-foot and outside-of-the-foot passes, touching the ball lightly in order to keep it close to your feet and therefore within your control. When an opposing player approaches, keep the ball on the side away from him (this is called screening).

When dribbling, you should keep your head up so as to be able to determine the best moment for a safe pass or a shot on goal.

Once you have learned dribbling with the inside and outside of the foot, you can try dribbling with the instep.

Dribbling with the Inside of the Foot

Push the ball with the inner side of the foot, toes pointing slightly upward. Keep your head up so you can look around the field of play.

Contact the ball midway between the big toe and heel. Keep it close to your foot.

Dribbling with the Outside of the Foot

Look up and around while pushing the ball with the outer side of the foot, toes pointing downward.

Do not let the ball get more than one or two feet ahead of the dribbling foot.

Tackling

If a team loses possession of the ball, the two ways of regaining it are by intercepting the other team's pass or by tackling.

In soccer, tackling is always directed toward the *ball.* Unlike American football, soccer does not permit the use of the hands or arms, and a *player* is never tackled. In soccer, the most basic tackle occurs when two opposing players are trying to gain control of the ball, that is, both playing it at the same time. This is a *block tackle,* and the inside of the foot is used to tackle the ball. Before committing to a block tackle, however, a player who is trying to gain possession of the ball should first try to get the other player off-balance by making a series of feints.

With the block tackle perfected, you can move on to other variations, such as the poke tackle and the sliding tackle. Timing, accuracy, and power are the keys to success in all types of tackles. Every effort must

be made to play in a safe manner when tackling. Remember, body contact in tackling is *not allowed.* The only deliberate body contact permitted in soccer is the shoulder charge, and although a charge may be used in conjunction with a tackle, charging and tackling are two very different things.

Goalkeeping

When watching a soccer match played by older, more experienced players or professionals, young soccer players are almost certain to be impressed by the actions of the goalkeepers, or goalies, as they are often called. They jump to intercept high balls on their way to the goal, or make acrobatic dives to knock away or catch hard, low shots. The last line of defense, the goalkeeper is often the focus of the most exciting and dramatic action of the game.

The goalkeeper is a true specialist. Agility, speed, quickness, and power are some of the qualities a goalkeeper must possess. There are many different ways for a goalkeeper to prevent a goal from being scored, and they require a variety of special skills. Among them is catching the ball, since the goalie is allowed to use his hands within the penalty area. The goalkeeper must also work on the techniques of punching, diving, and throwing, as well as the basic skills of a field player such as passing, dribbling, heading, and so forth.

There are two approaches for saving ground balls. One way is to bend the knees to get the hands to ground level. Only one knee, not both, should go to the ground, and there should be no gap between that knee and the ankle of the other leg. The goalie should move up and down in one smooth motion. In the second technique, the goalkeeper bends from the waist, keeping his legs straight and close together. In both instances, the fingers are spread and point toward the ground, with the palms facing the ball. For catching ground balls the hands are used like a big shovel. As soon as the goalie catches the ball, he should bring it quickly to his chest.

In saving high balls when the goalkeeper has to lift his arms higher than his chest, the spread fingers point upward, with the palms facing the ball. For balls lower than the chest, the fingers point downward. The goalie may not have to leave his feet to catch some balls, but for others he may need to leap high into the air. In all cases, he should move toward the ball and meet it, then bring it quickly to his chest.

Punching the ball with the fists is used when the goalkeeper is not in a position to save a shot with both hands, or if the ball would be difficult to catch safely (the ball can become very slippery on a rainy

Goalkeeping—Saving Ground Balls

In saving ground balls, the hands are used like a big shovel. To scoop up the ball, the goalie may kneel on one knee (never both), with no gap between knee and ankle, or he may keep his legs straight and close together and bend from the waist.

Goalkeeping—Saving High Balls

When the ball is higher than the goalie's chest, the fingers should point upward, with palms facing the ball; when the ball is lower than his chest, fingers point downward. In both cases, the goalie should catch the ball and bring it quickly to his chest.

day, for example, or an extremely powerful shot can sometimes push through the goalie's hands). The ball may be punched with one or both fists. Like diving or other techniques, punching should be worked on by the goalie in every practice session.

Any well-coordinated youngster can become proficient at diving by following a gradual progression of activity. Start out in a kneeling position, collecting ground balls as well as some higher ones that are passed to the sides. Eventually progress to starting from a squatting then a standing position. When landing on the ground, cushion the fall by a rolling action, starting with the thigh, then hip, then arm. The upper leg and arms act as "springs." Do *not* fall on your elbow. As soon

Goalkeeping—Punching

Punching is used in "case of emergency" only; for example, if the approaching ball would be difficult to reach and safely catch. The fist is clenched with thumb positioned against the index finger. The goalkeeper uses both fists together for high balls shot almost directly at him. When diving to the side, he uses one fist.

as you have caught the ball, get it quickly to your chest and secure it there. Of course, you should practice diving to both the right and left. Most school grounds have an area with sawdust or grass that can be used for practice. If you start slowly, gradually going for the higher balls, you will soon overcome any initial fear of diving.

In addition to these skills, the goalkeeper must develop the ability to "read the game" and show leadership. When his team is defending, the goalie must organize the defense and shout instructions to the other players if necessary. After making a save, he must start his team's attack right away by fielding the ball to a teammate who is in good position. The most accurate way to field the ball is by throwing it, and in most cases the goalkeeper will throw the ball overhand. The ball should be thrown so that the teammate receiving it can easily collect it. Generally this means throwing to the *feet* of the receiver, keeping the angle of the approaching ball low. Sometimes, especially if no opposing players are around, an underhand throw can best accomplish this. In this case, the goalkeeper may actually roll the ball to a teammate nearby. If the distance to one of his own attackers is too great, he can kick the ball, like a punt in American football. But with this method, accuracy is not as good.

Goalkeeping—Diving

A youngster can gradually obtain proficiency in diving by starting out in a kneeling position and progressing to a squatting, then standing position. The goalie avoids landing on his elbow and cushions his fall with his leg, hip, and upper arm, securing the ball to his chest.

Passing Combinations

When players have developed sufficient competence in the basic techniques of passing, ball control, and dribbling, it is time to practice *passing combinations,* that is, a series of passes involving two or more players. Passing combinations are used in order to propel and maneuver the ball around opposing players. The purposes of combination play are usually to move the ball downfield to set up a shot at goal or to keep possession of the ball until other members of the team can get into position to start an attack.

The simplest passing combination is the *zigzag pass,* a series of diagonal passes between two or three players. With a zigzag pass, it is important to pass the ball slightly ahead of the running teammate. It is much easier for a player receiving a pass to speed up a little to collect the ball as opposed to having to slow down, stop, or move backward, any of which would interrupt the flow of play. In the illustration showing two players, note how Ron leads Bill with his zigzag pass and Bill does the same when passing the ball back to Ron.

In the illustration showing three players, Pete has joined Ron and Bill. Ron makes a diagonal pass to Bill, who passes back to Ron. Ron then sends a long diagonal pass over to the left side, where Pete receives the ball and passes it to Bill, the player in the middle.

A modified zigzag combination is shown by Anne and Debbie in the third illustration. It is a combination of dribbling the ball and passing. Anne is in possession of the ball on the left side, Debbie is to the right. Instead of making a diagonal pass to the right, Anne dribbles the ball diagonally to the right side while Debbie runs across to the left. Anne, now on the right wing, makes a "square pass" (a lateral pass across the

Zigzag Pass—Two Players

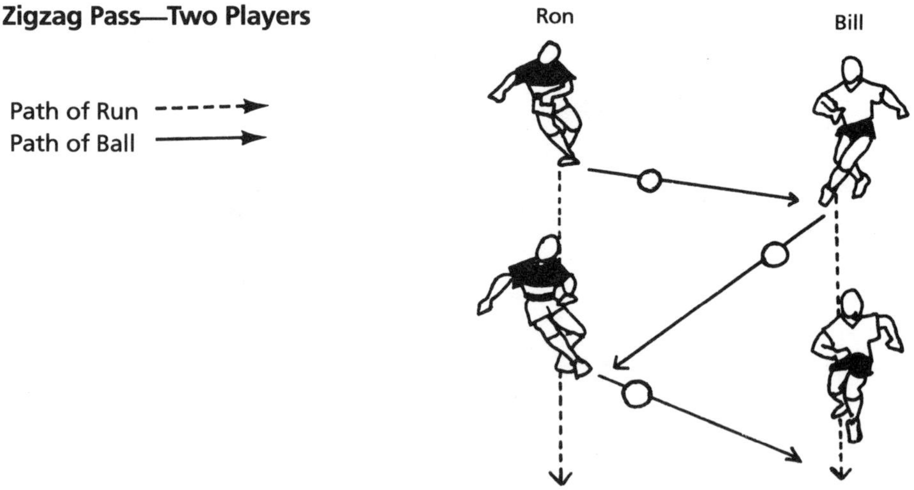

Zigzag Pass—Three Players

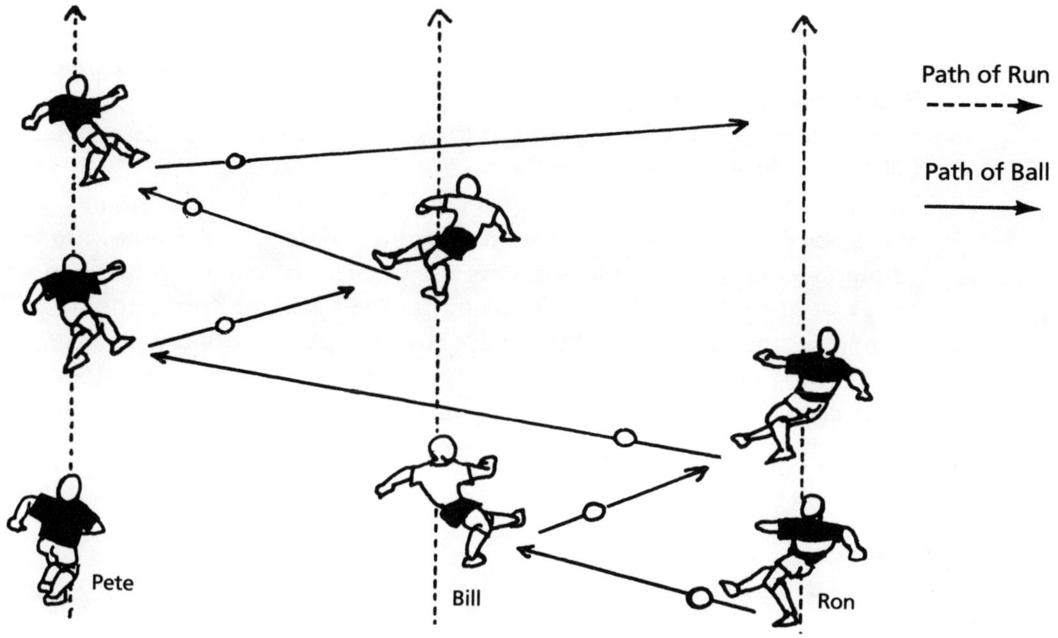

Modified Zigzag Combination

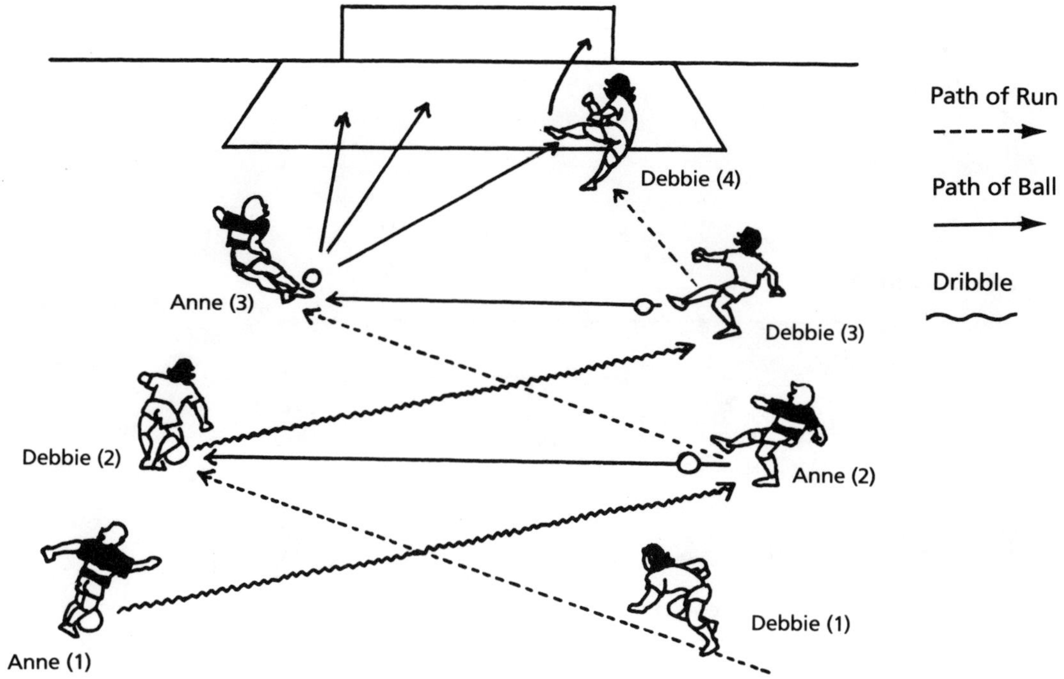

field) to Debbie. Then the same routine is carried out again, this time with Debbie dribbling the ball to the right and Anne running across to the left, where she receives a square pass from Debbie. Such passing combination exercises as these are usually employed to work the ball into a good position for a shot at the goal.

What are the main differences in the passing combination used by Bill, Ron, and Pete and the one executed by Anne and Debbie? First, the boys passed the ball, while the girls used a combination of dribbling and passing. But there is another important difference. In the passing combination that Ron, Bill, and Pete used, each of them moved ahead on a straight path, with the ball being passed back and forth among them in a zigzag pattern. If this were the only pattern followed in a real game, however, it would be fairly easy for defenders to position themselves in the path of such attackers. Their moves are predictable. But in the combination illustrated by Anne and Debbie, the players are

Wall Pass—Variation 1

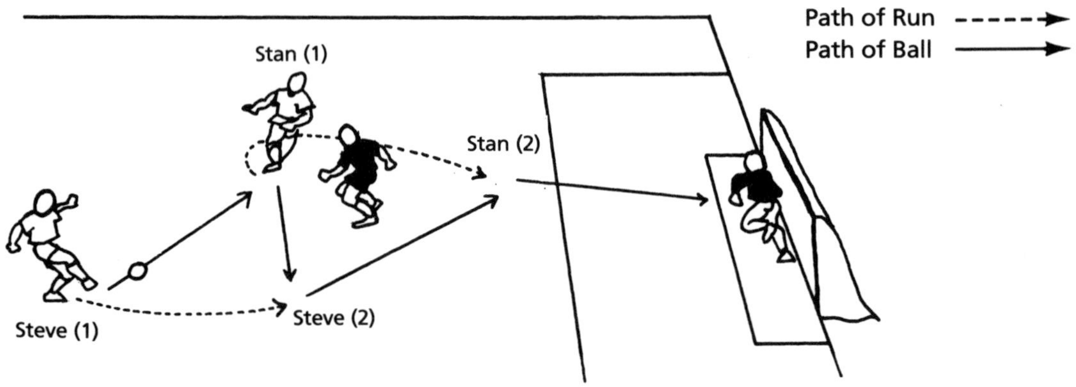

Wall Pass—Variation 2

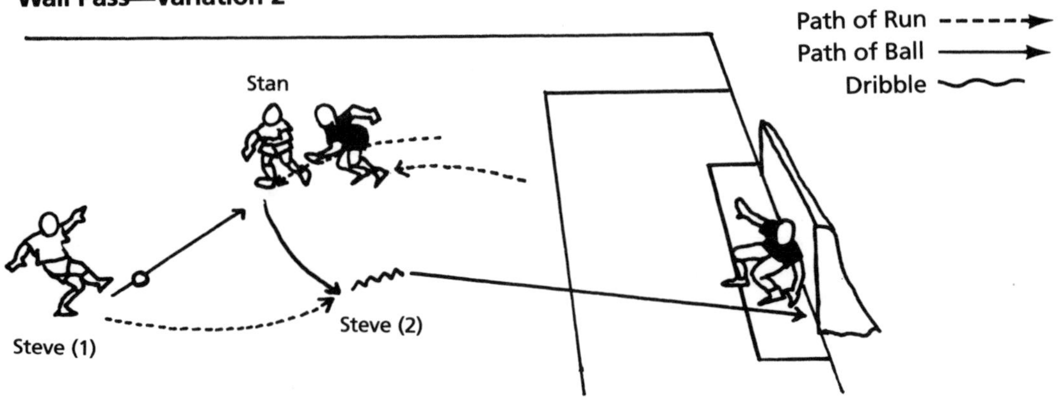

constantly switching their positions, which is confusing to defenders, who cannot anticipate where the ball or the players will be.

The passing combinations just described involved only the attacking players. Obviously, passing the ball and moving it downfield against opposing players is more difficult. One of the best ways to beat an opponent who is covering you tightly is the *wall pass.* Sometimes called the one-two, the wall pass can be compared to the give-and-go in basketball. In its most basic form, it is a two-pass combination in which one player sends a short pass to a teammate, who plays the ball direct (without first controlling it), changing the direction of the ball as if it had been deflected off a wall.

In the illustrations Steve and Stan show how to use the wall pass to trick a defender. In the first variation, Steve passes to Stan. He knows the defender covering Stan will quickly approach and tackle for the ball; he also knows that he is the only player to whom Stan can pass. If Steve stays in the location from where he passed, the play will not progress toward the other goal, so he runs forward. Stan passes into the open space ahead of Steve's run, then turns away from the defender and moves around him toward the goal. Steve plays a pass direct into the open space ahead of Stan, who shoots at goal. Steve acted as a "wall" for the pass from Stan.

In the second variation of the wall pass, the defender covers Stan very tightly. After Steve passes to Stan, Stan passes direct into the open space ahead of Steve, who decides to control the ball and shoot at goal, because Stan cannot get away from his defender. In this case, Stan acted as a wall for Steve.

The wall pass is used only in a small area, and the passes in this combination must be made very quickly. The surprise element and quick, precise passing are the secrets for success.

These examples of passing combinations are just a few of the basic forms of teamwork. There are several important elements in combination play: correct timing of a pass, change in direction, change in speed, and adjustment to the actions of an opponent.

Passing combinations help to move the ball while at the same time keeping it away from opposing players. The idea, of course, is to move the ball in the right direction and follow up with a shot at goal. A team has a much better chance to maintain possession of the ball and take it downfield with combination play.

As a player develops and improves the basic skills, he or she will need to work on and then perfect various passing combinations. Continuous work and practice are required because passing combinations are not set patterns. A game changes constantly, and players must adjust to each new situation and learn to improvise.

Chapter ***3***

Backyard Soccer

All boys and girls interested in soccer should have their own soccer ball. There are many ways to play and practice with it. Some youngsters have been known to take their soccer ball to bed with them, bouncing it against walls or ceiling, throwing it in the air, juggling it with their feet, even doing some goalkeeper diving exercises on their beds. If you are a youngster interested in improving your soccer skills, here are some ideas for you and your friends.

How often can you juggle the ball? Ball juggling is using the feet, thighs, or head to keep the ball in the air without letting it bounce on the ground. In juggling contests, experienced young players are often able to juggle more than 1,000 times, or to head-juggle 100 times. Juggling is an important exercise for getting the feel of the ball.

To begin juggling, you need to be able to lift the ball into the air. This is not as simple as it sounds because you cannot use your hands. There are two basic methods—using the insides of the feet to scoop and propel the ball upward, and scooping it up with the instep of one foot.

Once the ball is in the air you can begin juggling, using the foot, thigh, or head. You can use one thigh to juggle or move the ball back and forth from one thigh to the other. When head-juggling, the ball should be juggled from the upper portion of the forehead; you will need to keep your head tilted back and knees bent.

You can ball juggle on your own, but it's more fun with a friend or

Ball Lifting with the Insides of the Feet

Place the insides of the feet as close to the ball as possible.

Carefully and quickly, scoop the ball up by jumping off the ground.

Ball Lifting with the Instep

Point the toes of the lifting foot. Push the instep under the ball.

Carefully and quickly, scoop the ball up by lifting the knee.

group of friends. For example, form a circle with three or more players. Make your own rules, such as: three touches per player, then play the ball to the next person in the circle, always keeping it in the air.

Most youngsters will be able to find a basketball hoop at a schoolyard or nearby park. This can provide the apparatus not only for a good soccer skill exercise but an enjoyable game as well—kicking baskets. It is very simple. You start out by ball juggling, then try to kick the ball up and through the hoop. You can even devise your own scoring system.

The ball pendulum is a very effective device for helping you to develop the techniques of shooting and heading. It is simply a ball suspended on a long cord (one strong enough to withstand the force of

Ball Juggling with Various Parts of the Body

Start juggling on one thigh. Then juggle back and forth between both thighs. Let the ball land on the middle of the thigh.

Point the toes so that the instep is level. Let the ball land on the instep.

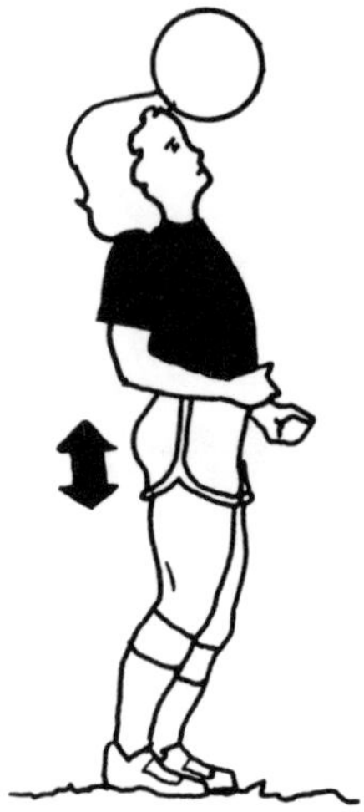

Tilt the head back and let the ball hit on the upper part of the forehead. Bend the knees and hit the ball with an upward stabbing motion.

Ball Pendulum

An excellent way to improve your skills is with a ball pendulum. Use it to practice shooting or passing with the instep and with the inside and outside of the foot—practice with the right *and* left foot. You can also gain confidence in heading—practice with the ball at different heights.

the kick). Most sporting goods stores that sell soccer equipment carry special balls, but if you can't find one right away, you may try using a tetherball. The advantage of using a ball pendulum is that the ball at its lowest position is not stationary on the ground but is elevated like a bouncing ball, the way it would be in a game. Once the ball is set in motion, its movement is predictable and the height will always be the same, which enables you to concentrate more on the details of the kicking or heading technique being practiced.

A ball pendulum can be hung from a tree, a basketball hoop, a pipe in the basement—just about anywhere—but the longer the cord, the more realistic the path of the ball. The cord should ideally be about 25 feet long, but it could be shorter. In any case, the height of the ball should be adjustable: very low (just barely above the ground) for shooting, passing, and ball control practice; knee-high or thigh-high for shooting exercises simulating volley kicks; head-high for beginner heading practice; higher than the head for leaping headers and for goalkeeper punching exercises.

Another fundamental exercise is to simply kick a ball against a wall from about five yards away. As it rolls back toward you, scoop it up lightly with your foot so that it comes to rest on your instep. Hold it there for three seconds.

A wall is an excellent partner for practice. You can shoot a ball against it or head one against it to improve your shooting and passing skills. Mark a circle or square with chalk or adhesive tape and try to shoot the ball into it from various distances and angles. You can do this with a friend, shooting alternately and allowing the ball to bounce only once after it hits the wall. The winner is the one with fewer misses.

Schoolyards, playgrounds, and backyards are ideal for group practice

Wall Practice

Soccer Tennis

Shooting at Goal

or exercise because you will need an open area large enough to accommodate the number of players involved.

With friends or teammates you can set up a game of "soccer tennis," with three to six players on a team. The field, about the size of a tennis court, should be divided in the middle, ideally by a rope strung approximately three feet above the ground, but if that is not practical you can simply lay some coats across the court to serve as a dividing line. Each team can touch (kick or head) the ball three times, then it must be played into the other team's half. The ball can bounce only once between passes or headers. One team gets a point when the other team makes a mistake, such as passing the ball more than three times, playing it out-of-bounds, or kicking it into the "net."

Soccer tennis can be modified to change the pace and make it a little more interesting. Instead of playing the ball over the rope, the teams shoot *underneath* it, with the scores registered by propelling the ball across the other team's end line. The defenders near the end line may use their hands to stop the ball. A player can shoot only on a pass from a teammate.

"Shooting at goal" is another sandlot game you can play, and it requires only one other player. Two small goals, each about three yards wide, are set up approximately eight to 12 yards apart. Players alternate being goalkeeper or striker. You can take a series of shots with instep, outer side of the foot, inner side of the foot, or by heading (goals need to be moved closer together for heading). Count the goals.

If there are three of you, you can shoot at one goal from two sides with the goalkeeper facing the player who is shooting. Count the goals. Players should change places every ten to 15 shots.

Of course, with only a few friends, you can also play a mini-game. Mark a very narrow goal. If there are only two players, the player in possession of the ball dribbles it, screening it from the other player, and tries to get in a good shooting position by making quick changes in direction and pace. Play around the goal and shoot from all directions. With two or more players on a team, you should try to outplay the opposition by passing to teammates or into the open spaces.

You can also add a goalkeeper, especially if you have an odd number of players. Older boys and girls may add a little incentive and difficulty to these mini-games by allowing only two or three touches of the ball before passing, by shooting at the goal from a certain distance, or by shooting at goal "direct" from a pass.

These mini-games are a lot of fun, but they also can be demanding and tiring. A more relaxed game of soccer tennis or merely taking shots at goal in between can help you catch your breath.

Naturally, the most fun is to play a "real" game—with two goals, two teams, and goalkeepers. If you have at least four players per team, you can stage such a scrimmage.

Select a size for the field according to the size of your teams. The matches can be made more challenging by allowing only two touches of the ball before it must be passed to a teammate (or else the other team gets the ball), or by shooting at goal only from outside a marked "penalty area."

In between your playground soccer matches you might try a game of "team handball," a variation of a popular European sport. In this game the ball is dribbled, passed, and thrown at goal with your hands. You can run only three steps with the ball, then you have to pass it or

Mini-Games

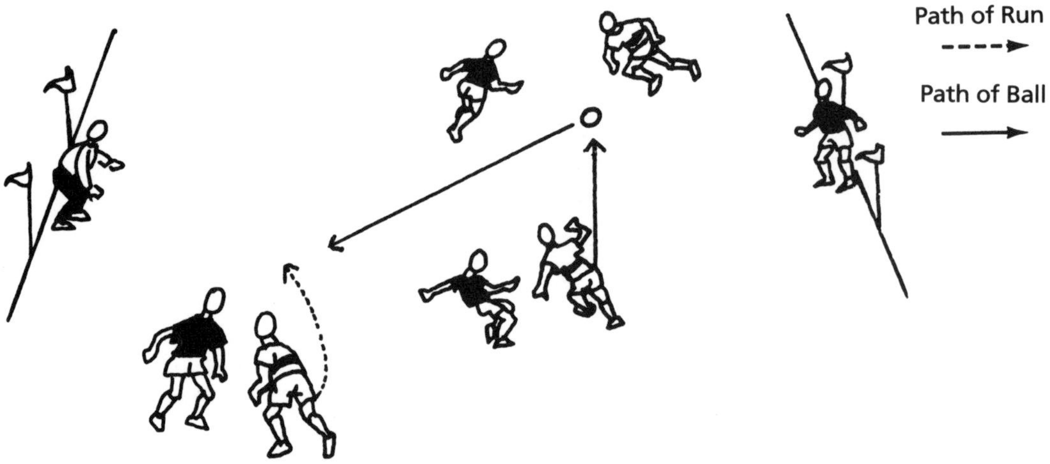

bounce it off the ground, as in basketball. Shots on goal are taken from outside a marked semicircle. This is a very fast game because you can make quick and accurate passes. It is excellent for physical conditioning, but more important, it is a fine exercise for getting a feel for quick positioning as well as movement with and without the ball. Team handball can be modified so that shots on goal are taken by heading the ball instead of throwing it.

All of these games can be fun, whether you play them alone or with your friends or family. In addition, they will help you to improve your skills and will complement the group exercises in your team's practice sessions.

Besides the fact that you will enjoy these skill exercises, it might give you additional incentive to know that many local clubs, leagues, or state youth soccer associations organize regular skills contests and merit awards programs. Sometimes there are even interstate play-offs and national finals! Ask your coach or local soccer organization for the information, or write to:

United States Youth Soccer Association
350 Fifth Avenue, Suite 4010
New York, New York 10118

Chapter ***4***

Teamwork: How to Learn by Watching

A player who is truly interested in learning more about the game of soccer should watch many games, especially those involving better teams and more experienced players. No doubt there are teams in your area that play a good brand of soccer. The top teams in adult amateur or semiprofessional leagues or in collegiate soccer always have talented players and can offer exciting game action. If you are fortunate enough to reside in an area that has a professional team, be sure to watch those games, either on television or, better yet, at the stadium, where you can be part of an enthusiastic crowd. Attending a soccer game enables you to follow the action on the *entire* field, not just the immediate sphere of action that is the focus of television cameras. And therefore you will be able to appreciate the skills, speed, and teamwork of *all* the players, to see the development of scoring opportunities, and to understand how a team's attack failed.

What you see in a pro game or one simply involving experienced players is an education in itself. Teamwork, you will quickly learn, is the key. The following discussion is a general introduction to this important aspect of the game of soccer. By knowing the evolution of team formations, you will better understand modern soccer. A knowledge of team formations aids young players in their individual development by giving them a sounder understanding of the game and how it is effectively played through teamwork.

Common Team Formations

Before the 20th century, when the game was still a mixture of soccer and rugby, teams playing with 11 players lined up with seven to nine attackers, one to three defenders, and a goalkeeper. The game action was similar to that experienced by the younger age level teams of today in their first matches, a pattern best described as "kick and rush," with one player kicking the ball forward and the rest of the attackers following the ball's path. Solo dribbling by one of the attackers was the basic method of advancing the ball, with the majority of his teammates treading on the dribbler's heels, eager to take over once he lost control of the ball.

In the early part of this century, the game became better organized. It was found that bunching up did not provide very many opportunities to pass the ball and therefore to maneuver it past or around the other team's players (see Diagram 1). So teams began to use the width of the field more, to open up the game (Diagram 2).

The trend also was to keep some players hanging back behind the forwards to provide more depth and thus increase further the possibilities for passing the ball (see Diagram 3). You can easily calculate the advantages of this development by comparing the number of passing possibilities shown in each of the three diagrams.

By introducing width and depth and by designating players to take on certain offensive and defensive responsibilities, the pattern was set for the development of modern soccer.

Assigning the ten field players to three different categories of position is still the standard, although today the number of players in each group and their responsibilities can vary. The basic three are:

Defenders—also called fullbacks, or simply backs, and including the libero (sweeper)
Midfielders—also called halfbacks or linkmen
Forwards—also called strikers or wingers

The term "system of play" or "team formation" describes the arrangement of these three functional groups of field players. In

Diagram 1

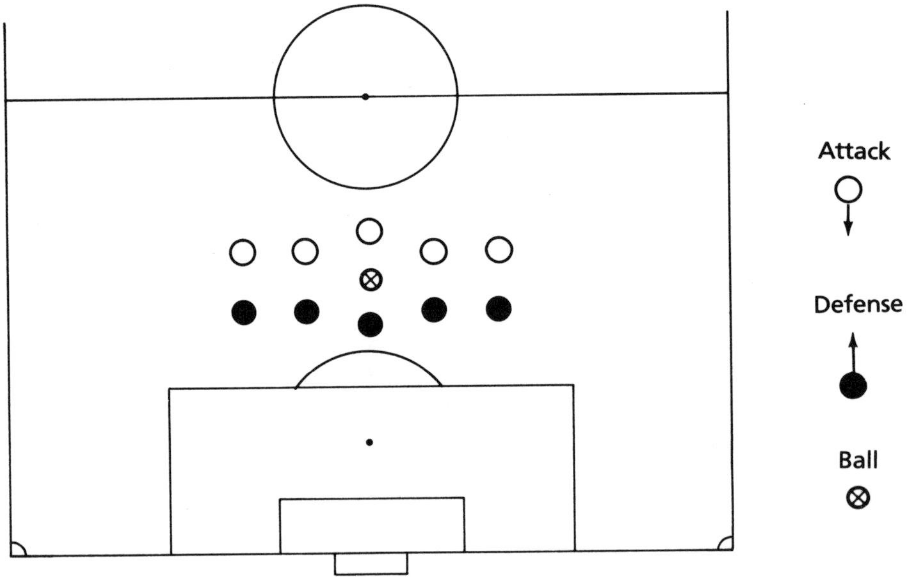

When players are bunched up, the possibilities and effectiveness of passing the ball are curtailed.

Diagram 2

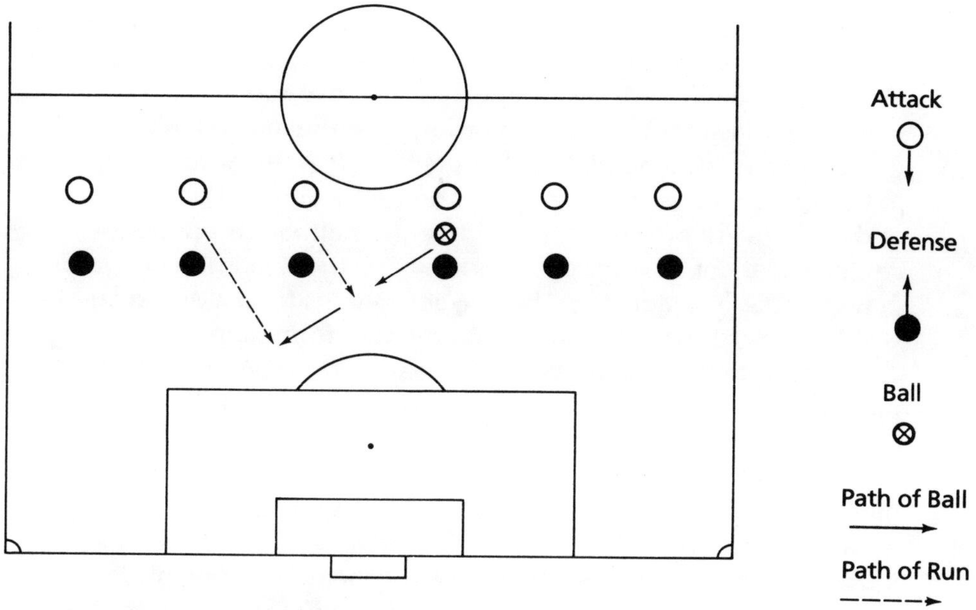

Spreading the players out to use the width of the field provides a greater but still limited number of passing possibilities.

Diagram 3

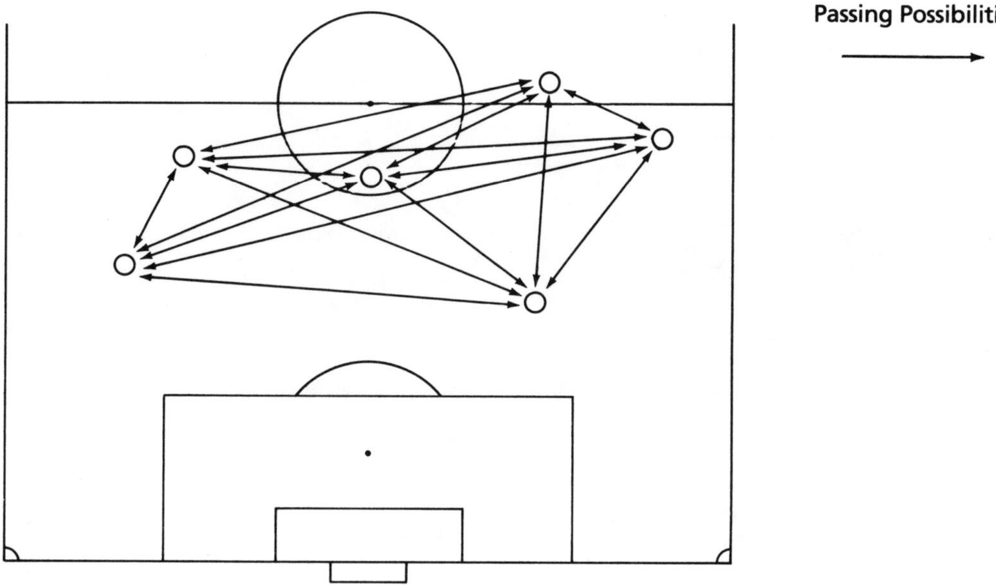

Positioning the players to take advantage of the field's depth and width maximizes the possibilities for passing the ball.

classifying team formations, the first number designates the size of the group of defenders (not including the goalkeeper), the second the number of midfield players, and the third the forwards. The formation shown in Diagram 4 is called the 2-3-5 formation because there are two designated fullbacks, three midfielders, and five forwards.

Another classic team formation evolved in the mid-1920s after the offside rule was changed, and it has been very popular for a long time. In this system more depth as well as better balance between offense and defense are provided when the center halfback drops back to a central defender, or "stopper," position and the two inside forwards play deep, as in Diagram 5. The player positions form a W and an M, which gave the formation its name: the WM formation.

It is important to remember when team formations, or systems of play, are discussed, that the players' positions are not rigid. For example, a team does not move up and down the field as a clearly defined W and M. For a team to decide to use a particular system merely means that individual players are assigned certain functions with the objective of achieving tactical effectiveness. The abilities of individual players, the special qualities of the dominating player personalities, the adjustments that may be required because of the opposing team—all contribute to developing a team's method of play.

A more recent team formation is the 4-2-4 (see Diagram 6). This system was used by the Hungarians in the 1950s but was made famous

Diagram 4—The 2-3-5 Formation

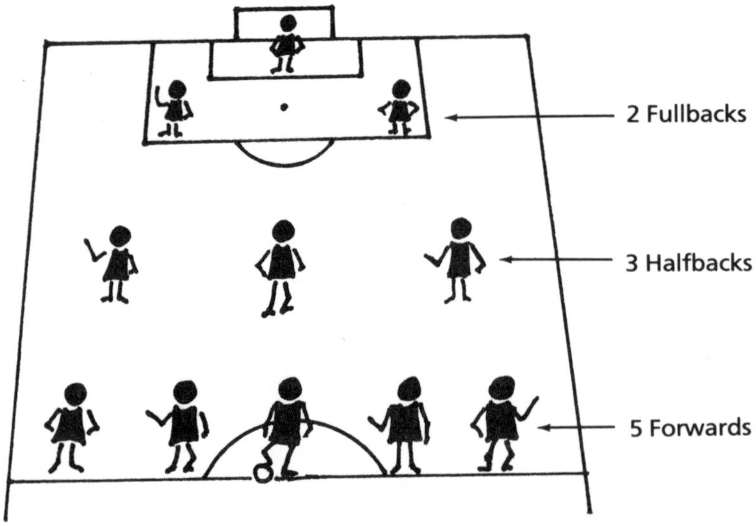

Diagram 5—The WM Formation

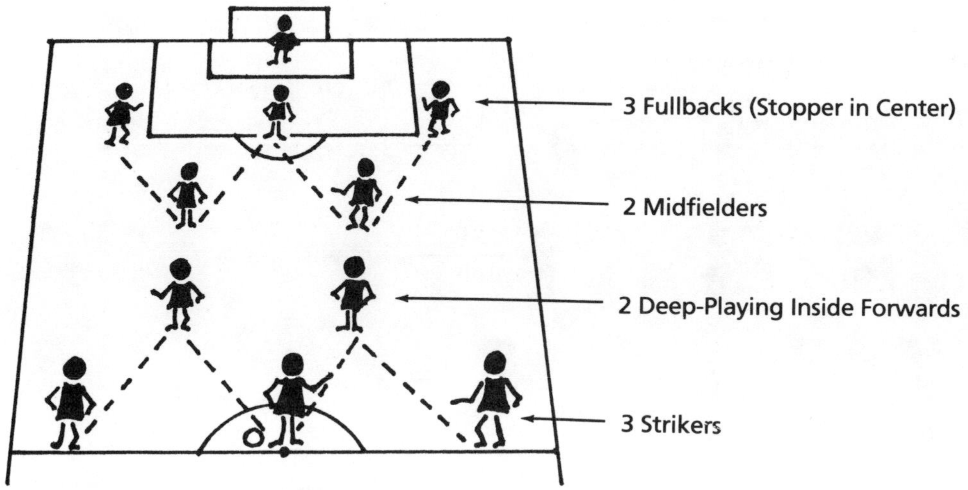

Diagram 6—The 4-2-4 Formation

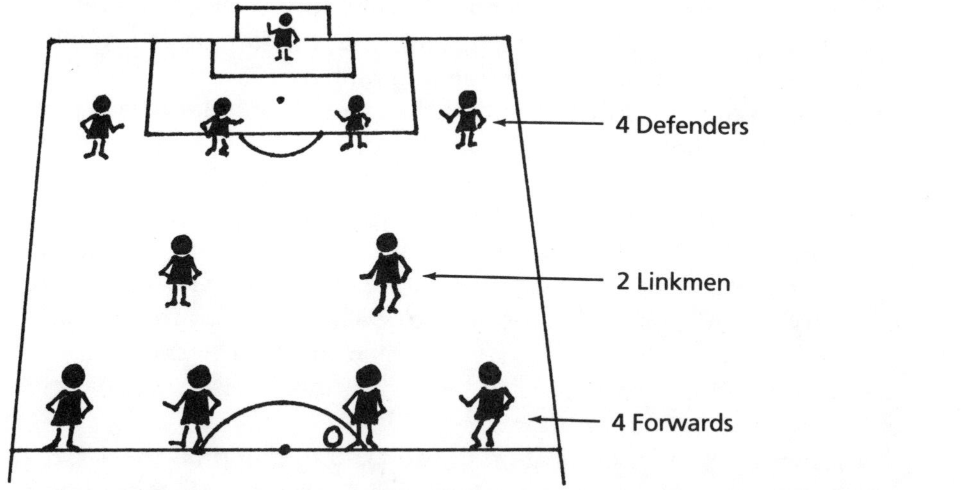

by the great Brazilian national team of the early 1960s. As the numbers indicate, there are four forwards, two linkmen in midfield, and four defenders.

This system is very demanding for the two midfielders. When their team loses control of the ball, they become an active part of the defense. When their team gains possession of the ball, the midfielders become part of the offense and are responsible for initiating an immediate attack.

Diagram 7—The 1-3-3-3 Formation

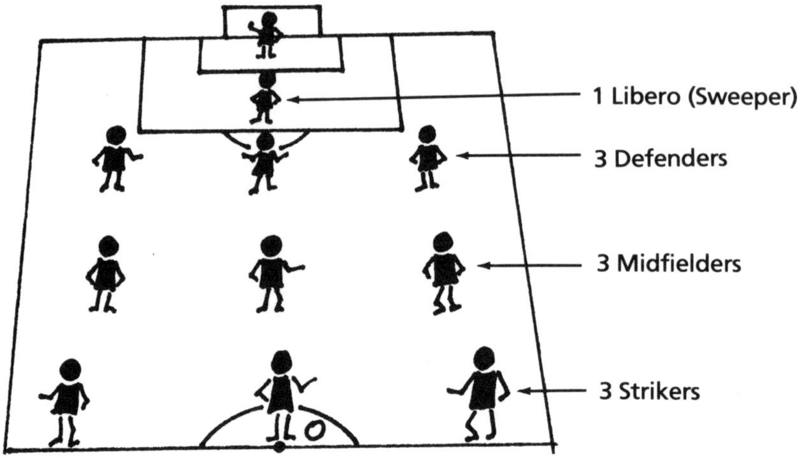

Today, the 4-3-3 formation and its derivatives are the most commonly employed. Beefing up the fullbacks and midfielders goes along with the trend, particularly in professional soccer, to refine defensive tactics. One variation that is often applied designates one of the fullbacks as a "sweeper" (or "libero," from the Italian); thus the formation actually becomes a 1-3-3-3 arrangement (see Diagram 7).

Provided both opposing teams use the same basic system, each player has a direct opponent, except for the sweeper. This player, also called last man or cleanup man, has the job of taking on whoever beats his defender and breaks through. Although the name sweeper or cleanup man implies that this player is only used as a last reserve, he has many responsibilities: "Libero" means "free to roam," and therefore he can be a very versatile defender. Just as the goalkeeper helps to organize the defense, so the libero can serve a similar function. Because he has more freedom, the libero can take advantage of certain situations and initiate quick counterattacks.

Another common modification of the 4-3-3 formation is the 4-4-2, in which one forward is moved into midfield. There are only two designated strikers, and so several midfielders are used to provide immediate support when the team gains possession of the ball.

Getting the Most from the Action

When you have the opportunity to watch a good team play soccer, what in particular should you look for? How can you learn from the experience? Here are some specific recommendations and tips:

Is the team *passing* well? Are the direct passes accurate? Can the player receiving a pass play it immediately, or does he have to slow down because his teammate didn't time the pass correctly?

Look for *passing combinations.* One of the most popular and most efficient is the *wall pass,* the equivalent of basketball's give-and-go.

Off-the-ball play is also very important for developing good passing opportunities. Observe the players not in possession or not near the ball. Are they "taking a break"? They should be maneuvering around, trying to get away from the defender covering them and into a good position for receiving a pass. While they are doing this, they should be *talking to their teammates* to let them know that they are open.

Talking to each other can be very important. Although a soccer player should have peripheral vision and know where everyone is located on the field, it is often difficult to be aware of every move made by a teammate. That's where "talking" helps, although it is more often shouting than talking. (When you call for the ball, keep in mind that you should use your teammate's name or your own. The referee may interpret a call like "My ball!" as unsportsmanlike—it could be used by an opponent to trick the player in possession of the ball—so say "Goalie's ball!" or "Pat, over here!")

You will observe that players in a good match do not run up and down the field in straight lines. They *change directions and speed* in order to make it difficult for the other team to set up a defense.

Is the team you are watching building up an attack by *using the open spaces* well? Directing a pass into an open space on the field, where one's teammates can safely collect it by sprinting to it, can give a team a sudden advantage. You should also note that a player quite often passes the ball to a teammate *behind* him when he is well covered and does not have a good chance to move the ball around a defender or to make a good pass forward. *Providing support* is an important part of play without the ball.

Watch the goalkeeper and his involvement in the match, even when the ball is not near the goal. His ability to *read the game* is of great value when his team is on defense and he must organize the backs. What can you learn from the goalkeeper's *distribution of the ball* after he makes a save? He tries to get the ball out of the penalty area quickly—before the other team's players have time to move back on defense. He will seldom use long-distance kicks, which are not very accurate, and instead will try to throw or pass the ball to a midfielder.

After a save, the goalkeeper sometimes passes the ball to a fullback on the side of the penalty area, who then passes it back to the goalie. Why? This allows the goalkeeper to move to the forward edge of the

Signals by the Referee

Play on— Advantage

Referee signals that he is using the advantage clause

Indirect Free Kick
This signal is maintained until the kick has been taken and the ball is played or touched by another player or goes out of play

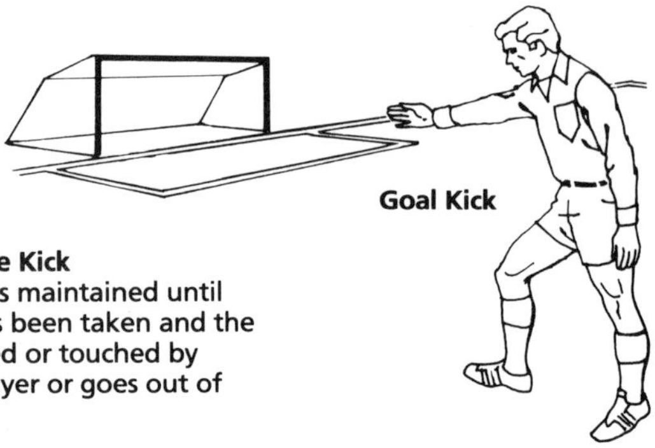

Goal Kick

Direct Free Kick
Hand and arm clearly indicate the direction.

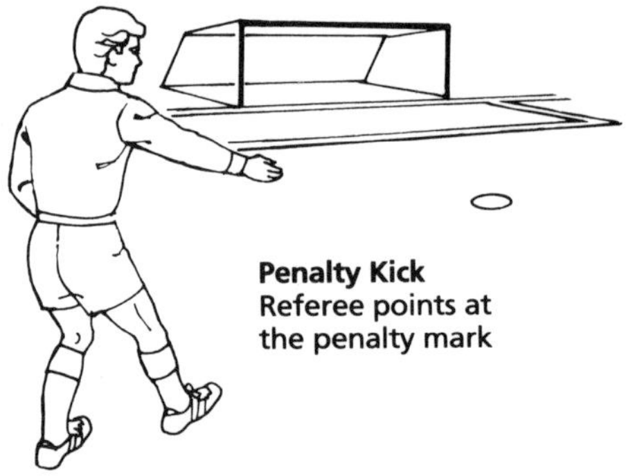

Penalty Kick
Referee points at the penalty mark

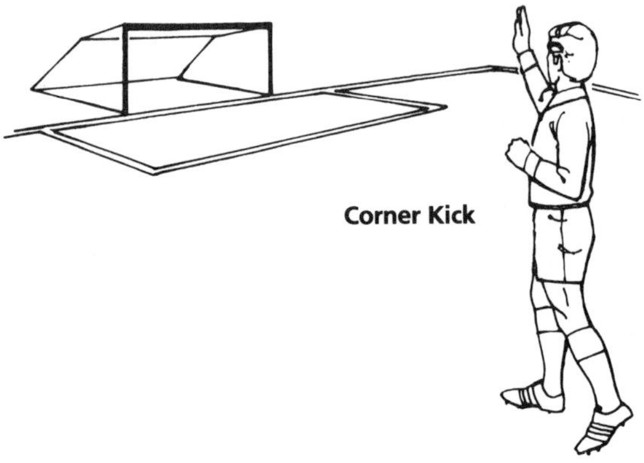

Corner Kick

Caution (yellow card)
or
Ejection (red card)
Player (or coach) is shown card and his identity is recorded by the referee at this time

Signals by the Linesmen

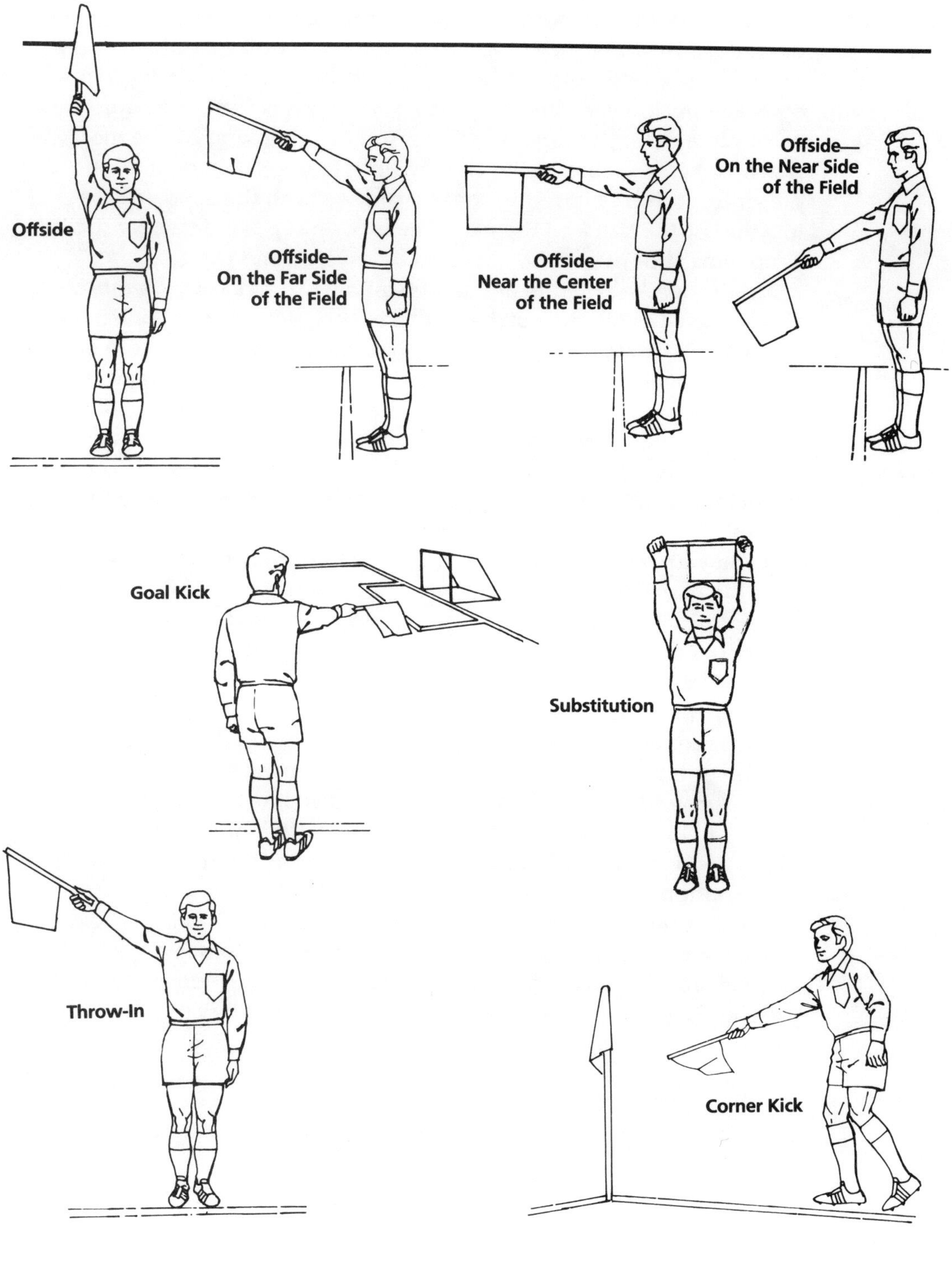

penalty area and from there make a long throw to a striker, usually a much more accurate method than kicking the ball.

When a team is on defense, watch for the *positioning* of the defenders. How are they *covering* their opponents? First of all, every attacking player should be covered. You will see tight *man-to-man* coverage in close vicinity to the ball. Farther away from the ball, however, a defender can give the person he is marking a little more space. But it is imperative, especially close to one's own goal, for a player to position himself so that he can see both the action at the location of the ball *and* the player he is covering. The defender should keep himself *between* the player to be covered and the goal.

A thorough knowledge and understanding of the rules is a *must.* How do the teams you watch use this to their advantage? For example, do they take advantage of the fact that the offside rule is not in effect during throw-ins or corner kicks? On a direct free kick, you may see the player who is taking the kick put the ball down and immediately kick it. He knows he does not have to wait until the referee gives the signal. And if he has the opportunity to catch the other team out of position, he will not wait until opposing players have moved ten yards away from the ball.

If you watch the referee, you will sometimes notice that he does *not* stop the match after an infraction but instead signals "play on." He has the right to let play continue if, in his judgment, it is to the advantage of the team against whom the offense was committed. This provision in the rules is called the *advantage clause.*

If you watch games at different fields or stadiums and under varying weather conditions, you will note how teams *adjust their style of play* to the conditions of the field and the environment. In general, passes on the ground work well on dry grass, artificial turf, or dirt fields. On muddy fields, wet grass, or even a dry field with long grass, teams are likely to use more high passes and long passes rather than short-pass combinations.

One last but important observation you should make about field players is that they all use the same basic skills; there is less specialization in soccer than in other team sports. In modern soccer, defenders quite often become strikers, and forwards will also handle defensive jobs. Players must have a good understanding of *all* the positions, not just one. In youth soccer, particularly in the lower age divisions, players should not play specialized positions but should have the chance to play at all the different positions so that they understand the opportunities and responsibilities of each.

Chapter 5

Mod Soccer: Being Fair to the Kids

Soccer, like any other major sport such as baseball or basketball, is played by people of all ages. There are professionals, who are experienced adults; there are full-grown youths just a step below the pros in ability; there are also youngsters, smaller and less physically capable, who want just as much to play soccer.

Parents as well as the younger boys and girls who participate must realize that a full-size field, more than 100 yards long and 50 yards wide and having a goal eight yards wide with a crossbar eight feet high, would be quite overwhelming to an 8- or 10-year-old. Just as Little League baseball players are not expected to play on major league–size diamonds or wield official-size bats, young soccer players must be accommodated according to their age and physical abilities.

Another important consideration in youth soccer is that in the youngest age divisions strictly organized league competition—with regulation-size 11-member teams, league standings, and so forth—is not always in the best interests of the participating youngsters.

Substantial efforts are being made today in youth soccer to offer structured competition that specifically enables participation at the young player's level of ability and commitment. In addition, the aim is to provide equal programs for boys and girls.

In order to create the best environment for learning the game of soccer, modifications in the size of the playing field, some of the rules

and regulations, and basic teaching methods must be employed for the youngest age groups. The result is what has become known as "mod soccer," short for modified soccer, and sometimes referred to as mini-soccer.

Bringing Soccer Down to Size: Some Recommendations

The governing body for youth soccer in the United States has set down guidelines to help individual communities and state associations implement mod soccer programs. The USYSA recommends that the regulation size of a soccer field be proportionately reduced for younger age divisions. The organization also suggests shrinking the size of the goals, crossbar heights, and field markings such as the penalty area, center circle, and so forth.

Without becoming too scientific, a simple size comparison can be made to provide the scale-down factor. For example, the average 18-year-old boy, according to the National Center for Health Statistics of the U.S. Department of Health and Human Services, is about 69 inches tall. Eight-to-10-year-old boys are only about 70 to 75 percent of that height, approximately 48 to 51 inches tall. For these smaller youngsters, therefore, the field dimensions are scaled down to about 70 to 75 percent of official size. The eight-foot-high crossbar is lowered to six feet, for example, and field length is reduced to about 70 yards. Diagram 1 shows recommended scaled-down dimensions for mod soccer. It should be stressed that these dimensions are approximate, and deviations can be made depending on the available field size.

There are probably several pieces of property in most communities that are too small for a regulation-size soccer field but big enough for a mod soccer field. In addition, by making minor adjustments, one full-scale field could yield two mod soccer fields (see Diagram 2).

Besides the field being modified for younger players, the ball is also

Diagram 1—Scaled-Down Dimensions for Mod Soccer

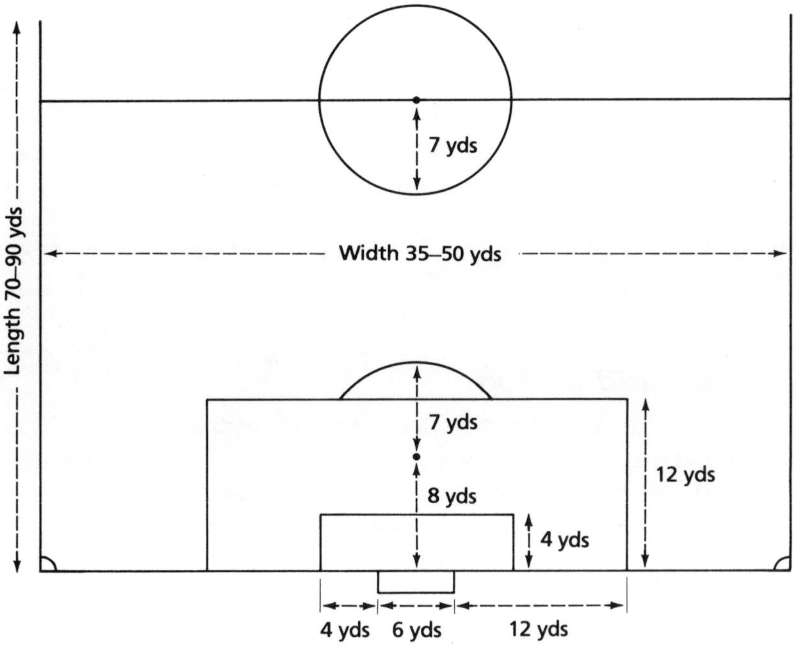

Diagram 2—Modifying a Full-Scale Field to Create Two Mod Soccer Fields

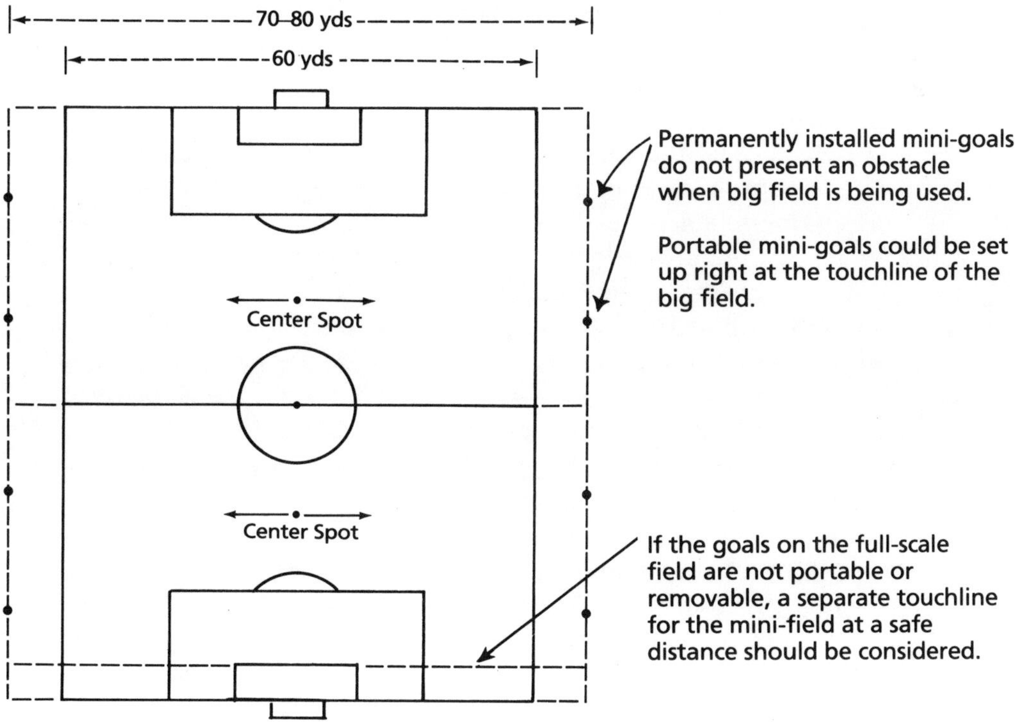

scaled down. Whereas the regulation-size ball for adults and older youth is 27 to 28 inches in circumference and weighs 14 to 16 ounces, the balls used by younger players are proportionately smaller. Players under 12 years of age can use a ball 25 to 26 inches in circumference and weighing 11 to 13 ounces. Players under 8 are allowed to use an even smaller ball, 23 to 24 inches in circumference and weighing 11 to 12 ounces.

Mod Soccer Should Be Fun

Teaching *skills* and practicing them in fun-game situations is the objective for the younger age divisions in youth soccer. The other two principal elements of the game, physical fitness and tactics, are introduced gradually in the middle-to-upper age groups. In order to achieve optimal learning conditions for younger players, contact with the ball (basic ball control, dribbling, and passing) should be maximized, while distracting elements such as game or league pressures and player specialization should be minimized.

Although this book is not intended to be a coaching manual, there is a progressive pattern for teaching and practicing techniques that should be understood:

- Introduction of the exercise, followed by demonstration and explanation of its game-related value
- Practice in small groups in "slow motion" or in a static position
- Practice at increased speed after reaching a reasonable degree of proficiency
- Practice with a mild form of pressure from an "opponent" to expose the young player *carefully* and *gradually* to a game-related situation

Practices should be made interesting and enjoyable by using a lot of fun-type exercises and games.

In most mod soccer programs, players are part of a "team" or teaching group that practices together regularly. Players are divided into small learning groups, in which they are taught the elements of soccer in enjoyable exercises covering the basic passing and shooting skills, controlling the ball, heading the ball, and playing as a team—the fundamental passing combinations.

Often coaches or instructors form teams consisting of about seven to nine players to play a mini-soccer game at the end of a practice session or on another day. The USYSA recommends that the maximum number of players on a mini-soccer team should be seven for children younger than 8 years; for 9- and 10-year-olds, teams should have no more than nine players. In both cases, the goalkeeper is included in the

recommended team size. At these ages, players are not encouraged to specialize in any particular position. Everybody gets the chance to play goalkeeper, defender, midfielder, and forward.

The "teams" or groups that a player belongs to are usually large enough to allow the formation of two or more mini-teams. In general, there is no need for substitutes waiting at the sidelines. If there are substitutes, they should be sent in and out of the game frequently. Every player is entitled to play a minimum of approximately half the playing time of the game.

The smaller number of players on a team means that each player is part of the action much more often than on a regular team with 11 players. Each child has more opportunities to play the ball, which means he or she learns and improves more quickly.

Youngsters are obviously not expected to know all the rules of soccer before playing their first game. Coaches will have explained many of the rules in practice sessions. During games, the action may be stopped occasionally to explain the rules, or to allow a player to repeat a throw-in if he or she makes a mistake the first time, for example.

When a group has mastered the basic soccer skills, the informal mini-games may be complemented by league games. However, the emphasis should still be on learning the skills of the game and not on winning a championship. The USYSA recommends that the results of mod soccer matches not be published, nor should league standings be kept. The emphasis for the age groups up to 10 years should be entirely on providing a healthy environment for learning the basics of the game. The children should be free of the pressures that organized competition sometimes encourages among coaches, peer groups, and parents. There will be plenty of opportunities in the next phases of the youth soccer program to experience the thrills of league competition, tournaments, and championships.

In summary, then, the major features of a mod soccer program should be as indicated in the following list; additional elements, such as teams and informal league games, should be introduced gradually as players get older.

- Coaches and assistants should have good teaching qualities, including basic practical proficiency.
- Regular teams are *not* formed; instead, there are learning groups

with a player-to-instructor ratio as low as possible (approximately five to one).

- Major emphasis is on teaching fundamental skills and very basic passing combinations in a low-pressure environment, employing fun-exercise schemes.
- Regular games or league competitions are not organized. Short pickup games on mini-fields should be considered at the end of the practice session. Teams are formed from the players of the group or from two or more groups practicing at the same time and location. (An extra set of T-shirts or player bibs should be available.) Referees are not used or may be gradually introduced; coaches can direct the traffic and stop the action in cases of rule infractions.
- Pickup matches must involve every player, leaving no one at the sidelines for more than half the playing time.
- Parent spectators should not interfere; they should refrain from criticizing anyone and should minimize cheering.

Mod soccer is a good introduction to the sport. It not only teaches fundamental individual skills and basic teamwork but also combines the game of soccer with social skills, a sense of achievement, self-reliance, and emotional stability. Players who have been taught in mod soccer programs are well prepared for the game's more challenging adventures and are usually most anxious to continue to develop in the sport.

A summary of USYSA-recommended modifications as they apply to the Laws of the Game is provided in the Appendix. Further information regarding youth soccer, such as pamphlets with recommendations for mod soccer programs, scaled-down field dimensions, and other aspects of this modified version of the game, is available from the USYSA. It should be kept in mind, however, that these are not rigid rules but instead are merely guidelines to be adapted to each particular situation.

Stages of Youth Development

Any well-thought-out youth soccer program bears in mind the physical and psychological capabilities of the youngsters and does not impose unrealistic expectations on them. Although the majority of volunteer coaches, referees, administrators, and interested adults involved in youth soccer are parents and thus have some familiarity with the phases of childhood development, it may be helpful here to provide a brief summary regarding the athletic development of young people, specifically in relation to soccer.

At What Age Can a Child Start Playing Soccer?

The official rules and regulations of the USYSA and of most state associations refer to Under 8 as the lowest age division. This basically reflects the assumption that a child begins to be exposed to organized sports when he or she enters the first grade of elementary school. This has been the case for most youth soccer programs.

With the increasing popularity of the sport, soccer balls can be found in many homes today. Younger children are being taken to practices and games to watch their older brothers or sisters play. And soccer has become for those very young children a favorite game in backyards, on playgrounds, and at family picnics. So it does not come as a surprise when parents decide to implement special soccer "programs," even for prekindergarten toddlers. These activities usually follow the philosophy of mod soccer but with much less emphasis on organized practice and more on fun.

Ages 5 to 8

Children in the Under 8 bracket are free spirits. They want to put the ball into the goal, *any* goal (they will not always look for the goal of the opposition), and they want to do it themselves. They have little appreciation for teamwork, nor are they very receptive to structured training. They may respect a person who acts as a "coach," but not for long—they just want to play. Coaches and parents supervising the activities must therefore be quite inventive in making the playing sessions interesting. Children in this age group have a short attention span. They enjoy movement, so soccer-related children's games and brief mini-soccer matches are ideally suited for them. It is recommended that children at this age level participate in two practice sessions a week, each about 45 minutes in duration, and one mini-game (about seven players per side playing two 15-minute halves).

Equipment requirements are minimal. There is no need for uniforms, special soccer shoes, or even warm-up suits. Youngsters may wear anything that is comfortable. Sneakers do the job, although soccer shoes are a good idea if the fields used are often wet and therefore slippery. As mentioned earlier, all children should wear the same type shoes; "mixing" sneakers and soccer shoes in a group can be dangerous. In some clubs or leagues, children are given simple T-shirts with the logo of the organization as a souvenir, a good approach for fostering the idea of belonging.

Official field markings are not required, but dividing the space available into smaller rectangles, or grids, for the soccer-related games will help the players to gradually develop a sense for field area. Fiber-reinforced plastic balls of appropriate size and weight should be used.

Ages 8 to 10

The 8-to-10 age group are still in a phase of accelerated growth of the legs, and the organs, muscle tissue, and cardiorespiratory system are better developed. The ability to perform motor skills improves, and the child's attention span increases. However, the response to structured training programs is still fairly low. Coaches should also be aware that the physical capabilities and stamina of the young players in this age group are significantly less than those of players in their teens.

The teaching program at this level includes exercises for improving the basic individual skills and the development of simple passing combinations. Small grids are used for small-sided games (for example, 2 players versus 2, or 3 V 3) that appeal to the players' eagerness for learning and their more pronounced enjoyment of movement. Suitable warm-up exercises should also be part of the program, but coaches should be careful to avoid excessive weight-bearing exercises, which could damage the growing ends of the bone structure.

The training program should be limited each week to two practice sessions of less than an hour each and one game (seven to nine players per side, two 25-minute halves).

Equipment needs can still be kept to a minimum, especially if the organization operates these age groups under the mod soccer concept. Games should be played on scaled-down fields with official markings and small goals.

Ages 10 to 12

Players in the 10-to-12 age group are said to be well balanced physiologically and mentally. They enjoy competition. Their sense of teamwork is dramatically improved, and they are eager to better their individual and team skills.

The teaching program includes refinements of the basic individual skills with more emphasis on power (for example, in shooting at goal) and should introduce other skills not taught before, such as tackling. There is more emphasis on game-type pressure in small-sided exercises (3 V 3, 4 V 4, and 5 V 5). Conditioning exercises for improvements in endurance and speed are gradually introduced. Providing a solid understanding of the Laws of the Game and teaching individual and group tactics are part of the coaching program. Play with a teammate and utilization of open spaces become important parts of the practice sessions in 2 V 1 and 3 V 1 exercises in a restricted area.

The training program should not exceed two sessions of up to 90 minutes per week and one league game (nine to 11 a side, 30- or 35-minute halves).

By the age of 12 a player should have completed his or her

fundamental training and show some proficiency in individual techniques, adapting to the requirements of individual and group tactics, and performing under game conditions.

Ages 12 to 16

Players in the younger years of the 12-to-16 age group are entering the first phases of puberty. Coaches should be aware of the mental unrest that usually accompanies this development. Growth and maturity-level differences among the youngsters become more significant and are even more pronounced between the two sexes. Players become increasingly interested in peer groups and in obtaining peer approval.

Differences in physical development and level of motivation and dedication must be taken into consideration by both coaches and administrators of a program, for example, by grouping players on teams according to their degree of commitment.

The teaching program should include exercises directed at the development of the player's technique under pressure from an opposing player and within restrictions of area (field) and time. A thorough knowledge of the principles of play and team tactics is expected of the older players in this age bracket. More strenuous conditioning exercises are introduced, and they are gradually made more demanding.

Athletically inclined youngsters are often involved in school sports as well as club soccer. Depending on the other sport, this can easily overburden a player and result in a noticeable drop in performance. Coaches should be aware of such situations and make adjustments to the physical conditioning program for the individual players affected. They should attempt to coordinate this with the coach of the other sport.

The training program is still limited to two weekly team practice sessions, about 90 minutes each, and one league game (11 a side, 35- or 40-minute halves).

Players should be directed to work out on their own, using the ball pendulum, or with a group of fellow players. Audio-visual aids can be introduced to supplement the field workouts and may encompass simple chalkboard explanations, training films, or videotapes of a league game.

Ages 16 to 19

Players 16 to 19 years of age are in their second, psychic, phase of puberty. Their physical growth rate decelerates. They are beginning to discover their own personality, to develop personal preferences and a personal style. They are becoming young adults and should be treated accordingly.

For the highly motivated player who is seeking an athletic career in soccer, this is the period for the final consolidation and refinement of previously acquired skills and a command of tactical principles under game conditions. Players in the top performance category, provided they have received proper coaching in their formative years, should be ready to make the transition to the top-ranked adult amateur, college, or professional teams. A structured competition program, in which highly motivated and talented players are grouped together and are playing in a league with other teams of similarly high performance standards, is essential for this final phase of youth soccer competition.

This does not mean that there is no room for athletes who are less dedicated to the sport, that is, who are less motivated to seek a career in soccer, who have other commitments, or who began playing soccer at a relatively late age. The general philosophy of the USYSA and its affiliated state associations is that programs should accommodate players of varying degrees of commitment and ability.

The training program for this age group should condition players for achieving maximum performance in their games. Perfecting technique and tactical principles in game situations is as much a part of the training as physical conditioning. Psychological demands on the player in league competition should be given special attention. Players should be assisted in developing and improving their own style, and team practice sessions should foster the creativity of the individual athlete.

Depending on local conditions and the level of commitment of the players, practice sessions of up to two hours each should be held two or three times a week. The practice plan may include specific training schedules for the individual athletes. A team should play one league game per week (11 per side on a regulation field, 40- or 45-minute halves). An additional game may be included occasionally in lieu of a practice.

The preceding discussion of the different stages of development of young players is a general description of expectations and performance standards through the full cycle of youth soccer. It should be realized, however, that various local conditions—climate, access to fields, availability of coaches, stage of development of the soccer program in the area, and so forth—may require substantial deviations from this outline.

Chapter ***6***

Coaches and Parents: Their Roles and Responsibilities

***T**he underlying goal of any youth soccer program must be to contribute to the healthful physical, mental, and social development of the youngsters. How well a local program fulfills this fundamental objective depends in large measure upon the adult participants—the parents, the coaches and assistants (who may be parents of children on the team), and the administrators and organizers—for they are the ones who must help to channel and foster the enthusiasm and eagerness of the young players. Most intimately involved with the children are of course their parents, who help to encourage participation in the soccer program and who influence their child's attitude toward it. The coach, too, plays a highly significant role, for he or she is the child's direct connection with the world of soccer.

Coaching and Managing a Youth Soccer Team

For the children, their coach is the central figure in regard to the team and its activities and the key to their individual concerns, hopes, and anticipations. The coach plays a very important role in the lives of the young players, with long-lasting effects, since children can be easily and profoundly influenced in their formative years. Coaching and managing a youth soccer team requires awareness of these relationships and understanding their importance.

The Role of the Coach

Although many of the management and coaching tasks can and should be delegated or shared with assistants, the coach of a youth soccer team should feel responsible for everything concerning the team, including its relations with parents and program administrators.

A coach must be intimately familiar with the organizational setup and the objectives of the local program and must have a good understanding of the scope of the state and national organizations with which it may be affiliated. Before making the commitment to take part, a coach should assess the program and determine if he or she can subscribe to the principal goals and objectives. A coach must cooperate with administrators and referees, promote the ideals of the organization, and set a good example for players and parents.

In the selection of assistants or a team manager, the coach must make sure that these persons are equally familiar with the program, share his or her views on working with children, and relate well to the team.

Understanding the expectations and the physical and mental capabilities of children of a given age division is another important prerequisite for coaching and managing a youth soccer team. This understanding, combined with good common sense, will pave the way for a successful effort and an enjoyable coach-team relationship. The different stages of a player's biological development and appropriate soccer activities for these phases are discussed in the preceding chapter. What follow are several general recommendations regarding the psychology of coaching youth soccer players.

In pursuit of the fundamental objective—to provide a healthy recreational and educational experience—a coach must strive to make practices interesting and fun. This is not to say that they can't be physically demanding or should lack discipline. To achieve this, practices must be planned well. It helps a coach to jot things down beforehand on a piece of paper and take it to the practices.

Even as a volunteer, a coach should look like a coach. A track suit or warm-up suit (shorts in warm weather) and a pair of soccer shoes do the job. Don't forget a whistle. Carrying a clipboard during practices is distracting, limits the coach's mobility, and can impede involvement in the action.

Creating a good learning environment also means using the positive approach in the coach's efforts at getting his or her message across, in motivating players to perform in a certain way. The two main elements are praise and encouragement. Criticism should never be negative but rather should be in the form of a constructive suggestion, which should be coupled with a word of praise and an encouraging remark. ("Tom, that volley shot was really powerful! But if you bend your upper body a

bit more forward, you'll keep your shot lower and put it in the goal easily next time. Hang in there! Keep working on it!") Depending on the age group of the players, constructive criticism can be used in reference to actual match situations, but this should be limited to practice sessions or brief team discussions after a game and should again be combined with words of encouragement, praising particularly well-executed skills or passing combinations.

A coach should be in a position to demonstrate individual skills. Attending clinics and practicing on their own will help novice coaches obtain a certain level of proficiency—to keep a step ahead of the players. It is a mistake for a coach to pretend to be better; the players find out anyway. Honesty in dealing with one's weaknesses will help gain the respect of the players and will indirectly help them to cope better with their own weaknesses. Aiding the players in reducing their fear of failure and developing their ability to deal with success *and* failure are important parts of coaching children. In this regard, youth soccer is a wonderful sport, greatly reducing exposure of the individual to high-pressure situations and emphasizing cooperation and sharing responsibilities through teamwork.

A coach should show that he or she cares for the players. Listening to the players, showing concern for their problems even if not always in a position to help directly, is just as much an expression of caring as the coach's willingness to put in some overtime to help those in the group who don't learn as fast. A coach should try to give recognition in some form to *every* player during practice sessions, with a personal comment (using the positive approach) about their performance.

Showing respect to every player on the team is important to the individual and for team spirit. However, this principle applies equally to the other persons involved in the sport. The coach must set a good example by showing respect to the coach and players of the opposing team, to the spectators, and to the referees.

Unfortunately, the referees in youth sports are often subjected to heavy criticism, sometimes bordering on insult, by parents, spectators, or even coaches. This is not desirable and is in sharp contrast to the spirit of the game of soccer and the general objectives of the program. Just as players and coaches make mistakes, referees can make them, too. The coach's attitude in such a situation should be one of forgiveness or at least tolerance. Disagreements with a referee's decision should not lead to discussion or a shouting contest during a match and in front of the players and spectators. A personal conversation with the referee after the game, or a phone call later, will be much better. The coach's personal feelings are secondary; setting a good example is primary.

Besides, games are won by displaying superior skills and tactics. They are generally not decided by a "wrong" call—unless a coach gets carried away and sets his or her own team off-balance mentally and physically.

Perhaps this is the appropriate place to discuss the winning-at-any-cost theme. It is the objective in athletic competitions to win. And winning games should certainly be one of a team's objectives in youth soccer, at any level at which league competition is part of the program. However, as indicated before, superiority should be achieved only by developing good skills, promoting physical and mental fitness, and preparing the team well tactically, *not* by taking advantage of loopholes in the regulations, poaching players, or taking other approaches not coincident with gentlemanly conduct and good sportsmanship. At the recreational level, a coach must refrain from applying psychological pressure on the players.

Along these lines, a winning coach should not demoralize the opponents by running up the score. Mixing up the positions on a team often helps to hold down the score, and the players usually enjoy the variety of roles. And what's wrong with exchanging players between teams if the score at halftime is unbalanced? Deemphasizing the urge to win is also a *league* matter. By not publishing standings or not using a system of promotion and relegation in recreational leagues, the general educational aspects can be better promoted.

A set of team rules dealing with the basic operation of the team, including discipline matters, must be established. A coach is well advised not only to clearly define these rules to the players, but also to discuss them with the youngsters, making sure they understand and accept them as an integral part of their sport, conducive to improving individual and team performance. Players will respect team rules better if they have been involved in approving them.

Penalties for rule violations should be clearly defined as well. It is not wise to consider physical exercises for punishment (conditioning exercises are already a part of the soccer practices). Depriving a player of something that he or she enjoys very much (a scrimmage during practice, for example) is more efficient.

Coaches should establish a good rapport with the players' parents. A meeting with the parents at the start of the season is a good way to explain the local program as well as the general structure of the state and national associations. It also enables the coach to present the objectives of the team for the season, explain what is expected of the players and parents, discuss team rules, hand out a schedule for practices and matches, and assign parents such tasks as providing halftime refreshments or assisting in field marking.

Such extracurricular activities as a team barbecue, watching a college or pro game together, a fishing or hiking trip, or a parent-player game at the end of the season can do much to enhance team spirit. Player-parent games can be fun, although they may result in lopsided scores with children of the younger age divisions.

Almost all youth soccer teams become a "happy family" comprising players, coaching staff, parents, brothers, sisters, and fans. Fostering such togetherness creates positive feelings and is conducive to good team spirit, but a coach should not let this get out of hand. A player must always be aware that the team is part of a larger organization. In addition to fostering team spirit, the coach must also foster club spirit. Where the organization implements a structured program, teams will be reshuffled at the end of the season, and coaches should not generate obstacles to player transfers within established club or league policies.

Team Management

Having gone through the psychological aspects of coaching a youth soccer team, let's summarize the general responsibilities of team management. They should be shared among the coach, assistant coach, and manager and should involve the players' parents.

Uniforms. Issue to the players, provide guidelines for laundry, explain the policy of where and when they can be worn, collect at the end of the season and turn in to club or league—all consistent with the policies defined by the local organization.

Balls. Take proper care of game and practice balls (rinse off dirt, dry, partially deflate when not in use) and make players responsible for collecting all balls after practices and games. Parents should be encouraged to buy a ball for their children to practice or play with at home.

Games and practices. Hand out schedules to all players and/or their parents with the following information: date, time, and location of all games and regular practice sessions; names of opposing teams for games; meeting time and place for games (approximately 30 minutes before game time for warm-up and a brief team meeting); parents responsible for halftime refreshments, field marking assistance, and so forth.

First aid. Some local youth soccer associations set up first-aid clinics for coaches and hand out first-aid kits. Where this is not the case, one

person who regularly attends games (and practices) should take on first-aid responsibility. Water and ice or cold packs should be on hand at games and practices. Coaches should have a signed medical release form for every player available at all times in case emergency treatment is required and parents cannot be reached. Coaches should request a doctor's release or signed parent approval when a player returns from an extended illness or injury. Know where to get insurance forms, if required.

Attendance record. Keep track of attendance at games and practices.

Player passes. Leagues usually require player passes or identification cards or official league-approved team rosters to be verified prior to a league game. These should be kept by the coach or manager (don't rely on parents to bring them).

If you have read this far and agree with most of the points presented, you qualify as a youth soccer coach.

Wait a moment! If you coach youth soccer, there is one more thing you must do: Smile!

Parents and Youth Soccer

The role of parents in a youth team sports program is affected by their love for their children. They want their child to enjoy acquiring skills and taking part in games in the company of other children. They hope that participating in such a program will have positive effects upon the child's general physical, mental, and social development. They are concerned about the organization's ability to provide a program that satisfies both their expectations and the expectations of their child.

Parents become involved in youth soccer at varying levels of commitment, depending on their personal desire or ability to help and on their receptiveness to encouragement or "arm-twisting." Typically, the length of their involvement is congruent with their children's participation, although an increasing number stay with the program longer because of a genuine interest in youth and the betterment of the sport. In addition to parent participation, youth soccer is experiencing growing involvement of single adults or married adults without children. The success of a program is based upon adult volunteers, those who are moving and steering things, as well as those who are less active or can only occasionally show up at games.

Just as a small number of coaches get carried away once in a while at games, so do some parents. Questioning an official's judgment, encouraging children to take unfair advantage, showing disrespect for opposing coaches and players, putting pressure on their own children—

these are just some of the ways a parent can err and in so doing adversely affect a game and the program as well as do injustice to their children and the team.

Parent spectators must set a good example in all respects. In particular, they should be friendly to their own children and their teammates, to the coaches, referees, and the other team and parents. They should encourage their child in sportsmanlike behavior; applaud well-executed skills and passing combinations; swallow disappointment in case of a loss; and use the positive approach (constructive criticism combined with praise and encouragement) in postgame conversations with their child.

It is evident in youth soccer that parents have learned from mistakes in other youth team sports and are determined not to allow the recreational objectives of the program to be overshadowed by the pressure to compete. In setting up a new local program, this can be achieved easily, without having to change traditions and existing policies. It is often a benefit in a developing youth soccer program that most parents don't know too much about this "new game." It is more difficult to *maintain* a healthy attitude, especially when structured competition and the formation of teams are not handled properly.

In the great majority of youth soccer programs the pioneer spirit of the initial phase carries on. Soccer parents seem to have an instinct for what is good for the children. They keep in touch with the coach and remain familiar with team rules and with the specific objectives for the season in terms of skill development.

Parents should take their children to soccer matches, be it senior amateur, college, or professional games. Soccer is a family sport in this part of the world, and this is one of its greatest assets. Look at the spectators at pro games: They are predominantly couples and parents with their children.

There should be a soccer ball in the household and it should travel along to the beach, a family picnic, or on vacation trips. Parents should play fun games and backyard soccer with their kids, or indoor games with inflated toy balloons. These are great for "slow motion" practice of heading, passing, or shooting. American ingenuity has produced numerous training aids in soccer. Many serious and enjoyable exercises are possible with a ball pendulum, and it is not at all difficult to build one.

Parent support is essential in the general area of "lobbying for soccer" with community, county, or state agencies, public schools, the media, and private firms. This lobbying can take various forms, from occasional phone calls or letters to "campaigns" mounted through the local soccer organization. Campaign objectives might include improving

coverage of youth soccer in the local newspaper, obtaining approval from the schools to use fields and facilities, or getting lights or drainage systems installed for extended usage of existing community fields, to name just a few examples.

Of course, parents have a lot of opportunities to assist and support league or club functions. The greater the parent involvement in these areas, the better the program for the children. Parents should not be reluctant to volunteer their services because they are afraid their time or expertise is limited. Making inquiries through the coach or league administrators, a parent will find that there are many opportunities for involvement at varying levels of commitment.

What are the risks of getting involved if you are a soccer parent? Admittedly, you may experience frustrations once in a while, but these are outweighed by positive gains—happiness, accomplishment, satisfaction, friendship. You may even end up on one of the thousands of adult recreational teams that are offspring of youth soccer programs. Whether you just mingle with other soccer parents at your child's games, or spend a couple of hours a month at committee meetings, or use your vacation to travel to youth soccer meetings in other cities or states, you will surely agree with the saying, "You meet the nicest people in youth soccer!"

Chapter 7

Youth Soccer Programs Under the USYSA

Soccer was imported to the United States at about the same time that it arrived on the shores of Brazil. In both countries it was initially confined to immigrant clubs. While soccer in Brazil expanded quite rapidly and became *the* national sport, a sport that actually had significant sociological effects in eliminating racial boundaries and uniting rival native groups, in this country it was restricted for a long time to areas with a concentration of ethnic organizations and, in some cases, metropolitan areas where religious organizations promoted the sport, again with immigrants as the main supporters.

Today, however, the United States is experiencing a youth soccer boom, which gains its immense strength and momentum from community-oriented volunteer organizations. There are youth soccer programs in all states; with few exceptions, they are supported, organized, and administered by parent volunteer groups. On a national scale, the United States Youth Soccer Association, with affiliates in all 50 states and the District of Columbia, has emerged as the strongest organization promoting and developing the sport of soccer among young people. The following pages provide an introduction to this national system of "organized soccer."

An Introduction to the USYSA

At its annual convention in New York City in July 1974, the United States Soccer Federation approved the bylaws of the newly formed United States Youth Soccer Association. As the youth division of the USSF, the USYSA is responsible for the development, promotion, and administration of soccer among players under 19 years of age. As part of this general mandate, the USYSA organizes and administers the formation of national youth teams, as well as regional, national, and international competitions. In liaison with the USSF, the USYSA supervises and regulates interstate and international team exchanges, to ensure uniform compliance with playing rules and organizational rules and regulations.

Another important function of the USYSA is to undertake programs that directly benefit *each* player. Two programs that fall in the general category of player development are the Skills Contest and the Merit Awards Program, both cosponsored by The Coca-Cola Company and its local distributors. Working with corporations in setting up sponsorship programs, the USYSA has been able to create additional funding for existing activities and to develop new ones.

Most of the USYSA's efforts result in indirect benefits for affiliated state associations and member organizations and the individuals involved. One example is the low-cost youth player insurance plans that were instituted on a national scale through the coordinating efforts of the USYSA. In regard to soccer equipment, the scene was dominated for many years by imported products. At the urging of the USYSA, the USSF, affiliated organizations, and domestic corporations and businesses, local sources for equipment purchases have been developed for the benefit of all users—soccer clubs, leagues, teams, and players. The

USYSA is also actively involved in creating and disseminating educational materials and audio-visual aids.

Player identification cards, provided to state associations by the USYSA, are aimed at fostering the feeling of belonging to a national athletic organization. They can also serve as player passes (used by leagues to certify player eligibility for team play) or for discount and promotional programs.

Belonging to the United States Youth Soccer Association is not expensive. In 1983, the annual affiliation fee per state association was $25; the annual player registration fee was 50 cents. These nominal fees have not changed since the formation of the USYSA. As a footnote to membership, it should be mentioned that the USYSA and affiliates follow the principle applied in other youth sports programs—that the youth players are represented by adults, mainly parents. Participation of the young athletes in the management of the program and in the policy-forming process has been discussed, but it is not seriously considered for implementation at this point.

The USYSA's direct affiliates are state youth soccer associations. Individual players, coaches, referees, administrators, and organizations such as clubs or leagues are members of the USYSA through their affiliation with a properly constituted state youth soccer association. Certain regional and national competitions, as well as training camps and competitions for select teams, are organized under the *direct* control of the USYSA. Not every team or player may qualify or be able to participate in these advanced-level programs. USYSA-affiliated state associations are charged with the responsibility of setting up well-structured programs to help their players develop and to allow them to participate at their own level of proficiency and interest, thus rounding out the national program.

The policy-making body of the USYSA is the National Youth Council, which is made up of representatives designated by the state youth associations and the elected officers who form the USYSA Executive Committee. The council meets once a year. The voting strength of the accredited state associations at USYSA meetings is determined by the total number of players in the association (one vote for up to and including 1,000 players; two votes for up to 5,000 players; three votes for up to 25,000 players; and four votes for more than 25,000 players.)

For administrative purposes and certain competition programs, the United States is divided into four regions, which are further divided into subregions. State associations get their charter from the USSF through its youth division, the USYSA, and are responsible for programs within the state as well as the administration of certain national programs. Because of size and other considerations, some larger states

United States Youth Soccer Association Regions

I–East III–South
II–Midwest IV–Far West

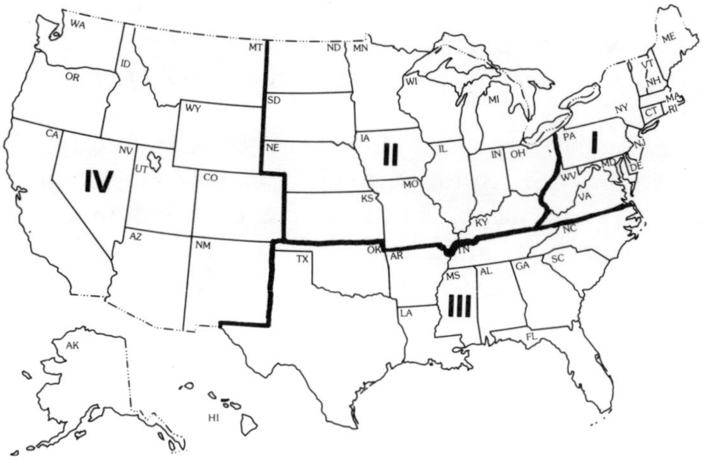

have two state divisions. Regional activities and meetings not only assist in reducing expenditures for national programs. They also allow participants from various locales to share their ideas and experiences, which benefits the overall program. Such meetings are also a good place to set up sociocultural team exchanges between neighboring states.

USYSA administrators and committee members are volunteers, mostly parents who had or still have children participating in youth soccer. As with other organizations depending solely on volunteers, certain weaknesses and inefficiencies must be expected. Limited financial resources—the USYSA has always been determined to keep registration fees as low as possible—sometimes add to these problems. Despite these impediments and growing pains, which are only natural in a relatively young program, the achievements of the USYSA's volunteer administrators at the national, regional, and state levels are remarkable. The growth figures reflect the quantitative progress: from just over 100,000 registered players in 1975 to more than one million in 1983, a tenfold increase.

The group of volunteers may differ considerably in their motives for involvement, specific near-term goals, and so forth, but they are united in their dedication to young people and their desire to establish and further develop a solid athletic program that is available to every child in the country.

Philosophy and Policies of the USYSA

Youth soccer programs under the overall auspices of the USYSA are geared to age levels beginning with kindergarten-age youngsters on up to young men and women 19 years of age. Needless to say, philosophies concerning competitive elements of the sport will vary in accordance with the physical and psychological level of development of the youngsters. However, there are some general principles that apply unequivocally.

For example, all registered players are considered equal and have the same rights and opportunities for development. Every registered player has the right to participate in games and, as long as he or she takes part in team practices and adheres to team rules, must be given the opportunity to play. The "unlimited substitution" rule, not common in youth soccer programs of most other countries, is important for implementing this policy, and it applies at all levels of youth play.

The *recreational* character of youth soccer, and its emphasis on encouraging each interested child to participate regardless of ability level, are the bedrocks of USYSA programs. In recognition of the fact that young athletes, even when provided with identical opportunities for development as soccer players, will reach varying levels of proficiency and motivation, the USYSA makes it the responsibility of state associations to implement a structured system of competition that will enable each registered youth player to participate at the appropriate level. The careful implementation of structured competition is designed to ensure successful continuation of the recreational program and at the same time initiate advanced competition and further development of highly talented and motivated players, our future stars in Olympic or professional competition.

Another proven element in recreational team sports is the "neighborhood team"; that is, defining teams by residential or school-attendance areas. Playing with friends encourages participation. This concept is very conducive to a healthy mass-participation program.

As has been stated earlier, girls are considered youth players just as boys, and all USYSA rules and regulations apply equally to both. The USYSA suggests that state associations develop and organize girls' soccer programs on a separate-but-equal basis whenever possible. In forming a club or league, there may not be enough girls or boys for separate teams or separate leagues. The solution, of course, in this case is mixed teams. Nonetheless, it is recommended to switch to separate programs as soon as that becomes feasible, because experience has shown that more girls participate under these conditions. At the administrative end, there is no need for duplication; both girls' and boys' programs can be administered by the same group.

At the national and regional levels, the USYSA sponsors separate competitions for boys' teams and for girls' teams. It is USYSA policy to classify mixed teams as boys' teams in these competitions.

The introduction of soccer for girls and the separate-but-equal concept described above were pioneered by several state youth soccer associations and quickly adopted nationally. The USYSA and its affiliated associations are thus leaders in the development of girls' soccer on an international scale.

With the promotion, development, and administration of soccer for young people, the USYSA and affiliates are striving to provide a sound athletic program for the community, a program that is interesting and fun, one that instills the satisfaction of team achievement, cultivates physical fitness and mental alertness, and teaches sportsmanship. The important educational tasks that will have a significant impact on the athletic, personal, and social development of the youngsters are entrusted to volunteers, many of them the parents of children involved in the program. The USYSA expects volunteer administrators, coaches, and referees to be aware of their role in the child's development, to respect the right of young athletes to have qualified adult leadership, to subscribe to the highest ideals of sportsmanship, and to make every effort to promote these ideals, not only among the players but also among their parents.

A Look at State Youth Soccer Associations

There are relatively few requirements "dictated" by the USYSA to state youth associations. State associations enjoy a great deal of autonomy in organizing their programs and setting up administrative frameworks best suited to local conditions. Looking at their development from a historical point of view, many states established their youth soccer programs prior to the foundation of the USYSA and therefore without any obligation to follow the USYSA's organization schemes. So today, USYSA-affiliated state youth soccer associations offer a variety of organizational structures.

What are the basic requirements for state youth soccer associations as defined by the USYSA? They must be constituted on democratic principles with equitable membership representation. Every player participating in programs under the auspices of a state association or affiliated organization must be registered with the USYSA and pay the player registration fee. State youth associations have the responsibility to provide opportunities for every player in every part of their assigned territory to play soccer at the developmental, intermediate, or advanced level.

State associations often evolved from relatively small, localized community programs. As they expanded into other areas, organizational subdivision was required to facilitate league operation and program management. To accommodate the average volunteer, to minimize team travel, and to establish ground rules for formation of teams, state associations took different approaches. In some cases, they followed patterns set by adult amateur soccer programs, in others they copied organizational structures used in other sports or introduced new systems.

Some associations have adopted the "territorial rule" from other sports organizations: The influence sphere of an organization for purposes of administration, overall development (including field development and usage), team formation, player "recruitment," and league operation is defined by geographical areas. This concept has proven successful in several respects but cannot be maintained rigidly in others. In the area of team formation and player recruitment or transfers, the boundaries of these territories can become open to adjustments. Therefore, in the developmental phases of a local program a certain amount of flexibility should be provided to cope better with these situations.

Two basic organizational structures form the backbone of a local youth soccer program in terms of volunteer involvement, player development, team formation, field development, and coach and referee training: the *club* and the *league*. There are basic similarities in both their administration and overall goals.

The club concept may follow classical European or Latin American traditions, but in the form generally adopted in U.S. youth soccer it is a new entity. Clubs in youth soccer are often organizations set up by parents for player, coach, and referee development and team formation. In most cases these clubs use community or school facilities for meetings and public playing fields for practices and competition. They are generally limited to youth programs, except for some clubs with a longer tradition, which operate senior amateur programs as well. A youth soccer club usually has to link up with other clubs in order to form a balanced league for competition. Larger clubs may be able to run "house" leagues of their own.

A league is by definition an organization large enough to operate balanced competition among teams. In addition, this form of local organization handles all other functions affecting players, coaches, field development, and the like. Of course, a league could still be subdivided geographically and administratively into several clubs.

During the development stage of a state youth soccer association, the clubs or leagues may constitute the only organizational subdivision. However, keeping in mind future expansion and growth, most states have considered or implemented another level of administration and program management, the *district*. The district obviously covers a larger territory, and its programs may include leagues for more advanced levels of play, clinics for advanced-level coaching or for referees, and special player development functions, such as district select (all-star) teams. Administratively, district boards and committees are necessary in order to perform the many different tasks of a state association.

The tip of the administrative iceberg is the *state* level, the state youth soccer association board with committees. Some of the main responsibilities of the state association are to ensure uniformity and compatibility of playing rules and administrative rules within the state association and with those of the USYSA; be directly responsible for USYSA competition at the state level or for state competition determining team entries for national competition; develop the game in nonaffiliated areas of the state; assign administrative responsibilities to member organizations; organize and administer statewide competition and educational programs as required or desired by the constituents; provide liaison to the adult amateur state soccer association, to professional organizations affiliated with the USSF, and to school or collegiate organizations conducting soccer programs;

represent the state at the USYSA/USSF level in all youth soccer matters; be the highest judicial board at the state level.

The policy-setting body or legislative branch of a state youth soccer association is typically the state youth council, composed of delegates from affiliated subdivisions usually with voting power in relationship to the number of teams or players in their respective home organizations. One of the functions of this body is to elect the officers of the executive board. The board, with the help of committees instituted and supervised by it, is charged with operating the various state association programs and functions. As indicated before, all these tasks are undertaken by volunteers.

After their membership rolls become large enough, most state youth associations lease office facilities and hire part-time or full-time staff for administrative operations, program management, and technical programs, involving such things as coaching, player development, or marketing. State youth soccer associations generally qualify as nonprofit/educational organizations under IRS code 501(c)(3), a status that is advantageous in many respects.

The structure progressing from state youth association through district, league, and club is typical for most states under the USYSA, although some states may use different terminology. The terms used here, however, are the designations recommended by the USYSA. There is a national policy that the term "federation" be reserved for the USSF and should not be used for any local organization. The national body also recommends that the term "association" be used for a state association only and not for lower levels of administration.

Finally, a list of committees at the state level may help to round out the picture of the functions of a state youth soccer association:

Administrative/General
Rules and Revisions
Judicial, Appeals
Registration and Automated Data Processing Services
Credentials
Public Relations and Publicity
Planning
Marketing/Sponsors
High School Liaison

Development
Player Development
Skills Contest and Merit Awards Program
Coaching Development
Referee Development
Audio-Visual Equipment and Material

Competition
Team Exchanges
State Tournament(s)
State Select Team(s)—Head Coach
USYSA Competition

Chapter 8

Organizing and Running a Local Soccer Program

If you are interested in starting a local youth soccer program, you can obviously try to obtain advice and assistance from existing soccer organizations in your area. This may work successfully in many instances. However, it is strongly suggested that new organizers get in touch with the office of the USYSA for more complete information:

United States Youth Soccer Association
350 Fifth Avenue, Suite 4010
New York, New York 10118

The USYSA can direct you to your state association, which in most cases will be able to provide contacts with people in your area who are experienced and knowledgeable in youth soccer, or may even send someone to assist you. These contact persons, particularly when they are familiar with local conditions, have proven to be most valuable in the initial developmental phase.

Getting Started: The Action Committee

In starting the preparatory work for a community youth soccer program, it is recommended that an action committee be formed. A temporary chairperson and a secretary should be elected by the group.

The basic tasks of the action committee are to perform exploratory work; to develop the outline of a program, including some basic bylaws; to stimulate interest in the community; and to set up a general meeting where the plans can be presented. It helps to assign specific tasks to committee members or even to form subcommittees if enough volunteers are available at this point. The following descriptions offer guidelines and suggestions for the initial study areas that should be addressed.

Organization and Administration

Informational material and other items received from the USYSA, the state youth soccer association, or other organizations should be evaluated. Invitations to representatives of these groups should be considered. In some areas of the country excellent program assistance may be available from independent organizations not affiliated with the USSF, and the question could come up, "Should we go with the USSF/USYSA or with 'them'?" In reaching a decision, it is important to consider not only the initial convenience factors, but also future development potential. Which organization allows the greatest freedom and flexibility in your local operations? Once the local program is well under way, will the coaches and players be interested in participating in national championships, in interstate or international team exchanges, in national teams? The advantages of USYSA affiliation will, in most cases, become clearly apparent.

Whether to call your organization a club or a league will not be discussed here; however, the area where the program is to be established should be surveyed carefully with the objective of defining "territories" for clubs or leagues. School districts or school-attendance boundaries may be useful, because these subdivisions are already set up taking population densities and youth growth potential into consideration. Statistical data and population trends can be obtained from city, county, or state agencies.

A name for the organization should be proposed and a set of basic bylaws prepared. Incorporation as a nonprofit/educational organization—IRS code 501(c)(3)—is recommended from the beginning, and preparing the paperwork needed to apply for such designation should be an important priority.

The playing season should be established, taking into account climate and potential interference with other youth sports and, of course, existing youth soccer programs in other parts of the state (you eventually will be interested in participating in exchanges or state tournaments).

A voting scheme will also have to be developed. A practical and proven system gives one vote to a team, with the coach, assistant coach, or team manager eligible to cast that vote in meetings.

Fields

The action committee member responsible for fields has a very important task, because without a field there is no play. First, agencies and organizations in charge of existing fields and facilities in your community should be approached. The person making the contact should be prepared to find resistance and a vast array of excuses—worthy of being summarized in a book of their own. This may be a tough exercise in self-control. It is dismaying to find how many persons and public organizations behave as if they "own" community property. But it has been shown that once a youth soccer program has been set up and is working fairly well, the "other guys" will eventually cooperate willingly.

An example of what you might encounter: The soccer clubs in one community had deliberated on the playing season and found that it would inevitably overlap with other outdoor youth sports. They decided to run the soccer league at the same time as regular football. Several fields (community property, of course) were graciously "given" to the soccer people by the football league after a lot of negotiating. Some five years later, the soccer program had grown so large that it was the football people who had to "ask permission" to use a few fields.

Experience has also shown that the special pioneer spirit among youth soccer people is inspiring and results in inventive thinking in acquiring and developing new fields. They will locate every acre of unused county or city property that is reasonably level, then use money from a candy sale or other fund-raiser to lease equipment to prepare the ground for soccer. After enough youngsters have joined the program, the park departments will generally move in and do the work.

In the initial survey of field availability, you should approach park departments at community or county levels, school districts, boys' clubs and girls' clubs, YMCA and YWCA, churches, local industrial or agricultural firms, owners of racetracks and golf courses, housing developers, and military facilities (the Army Corps of Engineers has often cooperated). Be imaginative!

You are likely to have more success if the club or league is willing to put in some work, will provide the goals, will set them up and take them down at the end of the season, and will do the field marking.

Equipment

Essential equipment consists of goals, field-marking equipment and safe marking material, and of course, soccer balls. Goal nets and corner flags may be considered an option—*additional practice balls are more important.*

To buy balls, you simply get quotes from stores or other suppliers to establish a budget input. Buying in quantity can save money, so ordering balls for the entire club or league is often a good idea. Using the same make of game ball throughout the league also makes sense. You will avoid or reduce problems and frustrations if all important details regarding the balls are specified in the contract or purchase order, such as circumference and weight in addition to the size number. Material and coating should be selected carefully and specified in the purchase order. The choice will depend on the fields that will be used and on the climatic conditions during the playing season (a durable waterproof coating will be needed in areas with fair amounts of precipitation, for example).

As to goalposts, you will find a variety of options ranging from aircraft alloy portables to permanently installed technical masterworks. There is also the do-it-yourself approach, using lumber or metal from scrapyards or surplus sales. Wooden goalposts featuring 4 × 4's for uprights and crossbars (where 4 × 4 lumber in 24-foot lengths is not available, two or more lengths of 2 × 4's, securely bolted together, can be used) are sturdy enough and will last for several seasons if properly protected (painted) and stored during the off-season. American football goalposts featuring continuous uprights can double as soccer goals with the addition of a second crossbar.

The deluxe or budget approach can be taken for field-marking equipment as well. Lawn spreaders can easily be converted by closing the openings (use solder or heavy-duty tape) except for an area in the middle corresponding to the width of the line being marked. Obtain a marking material that is safe and does not cause irritations in case a player with skin abrasions comes in contact with it. Agricultural gypsum is one possibility.

A nylon string should be used as a guide to ensure straight lines. Tie one end of the string to a long nail or old screwdriver, which can then be driven into the ground. This makes one-man lining operations much easier. It also helps to attach markings, such as pieces of tape, to the string at intervals of one, six, ten, 12, and 18 yards for measuring or pre-marking corner radius, goal area, penalty area, and center circle.

The equipment planning study should also include provisions for storing all equipment during the off-season.

Uniforms

The person or subcommittee in charge of uniforms should locate sources for the mass purchase of shirts, shorts, and socks in various color schemes. The budget approach might be to order standard gym shorts and tube socks of one color and purchase sets of T-shirts or soccer shirts

in different colors. The basic task is to acquire shirts that avoid or greatly reduce the possibility of color duplication between teams. One practical solution would be two-color reversible shirts; however, they are usually heavier than regular shirts and are not always satisfactory from a player's point of view. Clubs may consider making spare sets of uniforms available in case of color conflicts, or simply requesting that teams have an extra set of T-shirts of a different color.

Numbers on jerseys are good for many reasons, not the least of them being a kind of personal identification. Numbers can also provide relationships with soccer greats (Pele's number 10!). They should be used if it is possible within the budget.

If well cared for, uniforms will last two or three seasons. They should be collected at the end of the season, cleaned, and properly stored.

Finances

Cost estimates are gathered from all subcommittees or action committee members. One of the tasks for the finance study committee is to prepare a budget outline. In addition to uniforms and equipment purchases, the following expenditures should be included: telephone, stationery supplies, postage, insurance fees, player registration fees for state and national associations, field maintenance or lease (where required), fees for referees, and the purchase of rule books for coaches and referees.

As part of the initial study, the person responsible for financial matters should also explore the possibility of sponsorships and donations or other potential sources of income for the organization.

Coaches

Locating people with experience in coaching youngsters in soccer may be difficult, especially in an area where soccer is not an established youth sport. The committee, however, should not be discouraged in such a case. Most future coaches will be recruited from the parents of the players, and while some previous experience is helpful, it is by no means necessary. One of the largest state youth soccer programs in the United States was started by a man with a soccer background in "the old country" and a small group of parents who learned from scratch as they were put in charge of their neighborhood's teams.

The committee should try to find people in the community with soccer playing experience who could give some assistance to novice coaches. The possibility of introductory clinics through the state senior or youth soccer associations or the USYSA should be investigated. Coaching manuals should also be provided (available from the USYSA).

Referees

What applies to coaches in new programs is usually applicable to referees as well. Referee units are maintained by most state associations and may be called upon for clinics or even for providing referees. Fee scales and availability should be determined. In many cases, you will have to provide your own referees. A common and successful system in youth soccer has been to use the coaches for this job. A coach is scheduled to officiate the match preceding or following his or her own match on the home field.

Public Relations and Recruiting

The exploratory study must also address the "recruiting" of youngsters and the formation of teams. An important element is developing a plan for announcing the program and the days and locations for player registration. You should try to obtain cooperation from schools and the local media. For example, a pilot study to establish predictions on how many children at various age levels will participate could be arranged by distributing questionnaires at schools.

In order to determine the best approach in "getting the word out" once the program is defined, the action committee should contact the school administration (would schools distribute sign-up forms?) and local newspapers, radio, and television stations (would they publicize information on registration as a community service?). Other organizations such as the YMCA and YWCA, churches, boys' clubs, and the like, should be consulted regarding announcements and availability of facilities for registration day.

Once the exploratory work has been completed, a budget has been established, and a player registration fee has been estimated based on projected participation, the action committee should call a meeting for interested parents and other adults. A vote of confidence for the proposed program outline would be the kickoff for the program. The action committee, with the consensus of the attendees, could be put in charge of the organization or could propose that an interim board of control be elected at that first general meeting. The election of a permanent board should be scheduled to take place after registration and the formation of teams, using the voting scheme mentioned earlier, which assigns each team one vote.

The dates, times, and locations for player registration should be announced at the first meeting and then further publicized through the media. Sample forms for player sign-up are available through the USYSA or the state association. They should include a section where parents can volunteer if they are willing to help—as committee member, coach, referee, and so forth.

The guideline for the formation of teams in this new organization's first season should only be residential area or school-attendance area (neighborhood teams). Tryouts must be avoided because they would be discouraging to many children. A policy should also be adopted that children will not be denied participation if their parents are unable to pay the fee (hardship situations).

For putting together teams and for general coordination between the board and the coaches, the implementation of age division coordinators should be considered, particularly if the organization turns out to be fairly large.

Making It Official

After player sign-up and team formation, a club or league meeting should be scheduled for the basic purpose of electing a permanent board of control and appointing permanent committees as well as assigning "work parties."

Even dedicated volunteers may need an extra incentive to slip away from the TV for an evening. So something interesting or important or even controversial should be planned for every meeting. For this first time, it could be issuing balls and rule books to the coaches, assigning home fields or even game schedules, or showing a movie on coaching or refereeing.

The paperwork for incorporation should be processed soon after the first "official" club or league meeting.

A list of officers and committee chairpersons should be sent to the state youth association or the organizational subdivision responsible for your area. This association must also get a copy of the league or club bylaws, which cannot be in conflict with those of the state association.

The division of the bylaws into the categories of constitution, bylaws, and rules and regulations has been found quite practical. The constitution defines things that don't change, such as the name of the organization and its purposes and objectives; amendments are possible only at the annual general meeting. Bylaws define the administrative rules, and provisions to change them during the year (with proper notice) should be included. Rules and regulations are treated in a manner similar to the bylaws but contain all rules related to the competition aspects of your organization.

The administrative body of a typical soccer program and its basic functions are summarized below.

The Board of Control

The board of control can have different titles, such as board of directors or executive board. It should be composed of four principal officers—president, vice-president, secretary, treasurer—plus additional officers

who are in charge of certain important areas or functions, such as coaching development, referee development, player registration, and so forth. Of course, some or most of these functions could be run by committees responsible to the board. Six to eight persons has proven to be an effective size for this kind of volunteer organization.

President. The president presides at all meetings, is the general representative of the organization, and specifically serves as liaison to the next higher governing body in the state youth association hierarchy. The president establishes committees as required and appoints their chairpersons, subject to approval of the board.

Vice-president. The vice-president assists the president and succeeds to the presidency in the absence of or after the resignation of the president. The division of work between president and vice-president should be clearly defined.

Secretary. The secretary records and publishes minutes of the meetings and takes care of other correspondence, including notification of meetings and bylaw amendment proposals.

Treasurer. The treasurer deposits funds in a chartered bank, cosigns checks (with the president) for properly authorized disbursements, maintains accounts, publishes financial statements, and prepares or assists in preparing a budget proposal.

Key Committees

The following are key committee functions of an ongoing soccer program. Depending on the organization, it might be good to include some of them as additional board positions. Much of what has already been discussed above with regard to the tasks of the action committee would of course still apply to running your program.

Fields and scheduling. Makes field assignments for practices and games and prepares league schedules.

Equipment. Responsible for the acquisition, maintenance, storage, and distribution of field equipment (goals, balls, markers, marking material), unless this service is provided for by other organizations or agencies.

Uniforms. Acquires, replaces, distributes, collects, and stores player uniforms.

Registration. In charge of collecting player sign-up forms, verifying birthdates, completing and approving player and team registration forms, maintaining player transfer records and related subjects, and liaising with the state youth soccer association in registration matters. A special note: As teams progress to more advanced levels, eligibility matters may become more important. But even at the beginner's level, registration in general is an important part of organized sports. For example, evaluation of statistical data can be valuable in overall program planning. The registrar should also work closely with the insurance committee.

Referees. Sets up clinics for referee development, including short clinics for parents who are moderately interested in helping out and would not mind getting a briefing on how to assist as a linesman, and assigns referees to league matches. Where a referee organization exists or after one has been developed as part of the new program, some or all of these functions may be handled by that group.

Coach and player development. Organizes coaching clinics and certain clinics for players.

Fund-raising and sponsors. Develops, implements, and supervises fund-raising programs for the organization; solicits sponsors. Policies regarding sponsors must be set by the organization with the primary goal of assuring all teams of equal treatment for general league play. This can be achieved by putting income from sponsors into the general fund or allocating it to certain segments of the program, making sure that recognition is given to the sponsors in an appropriate form. There are no USYSA policies regarding the use of a sponsor's name or company name in the team name. But sponsors cannot be given a voice in operating the club or league.

Judicial. A judicial system should be developed, even though this may sound strange, particularly for a recreational youth sports program. For one thing, the right to appeal decisions is one of the fundamental ingredients in a democratically structured organization. And even if everything is running smoothly, there will be occasions when coaches or administrators want to take advantage of this right. The judicial system should address organizational matters, competition, and disciplinary action for individual players or coaches having been found guilty of violating regulations. Procedures for protests, appeals, and other judicial decisions should be defined in the organization's bylaws. They should describe the chain of command beyond the level of the local organization (for example, local—state—regional—national level) and should include a clause that no one may engage the services of an attorney until all avenues of judicial procedures within the structure of organized soccer have been exhausted.

Publicity and public relations. Develops and maintains a good relationship with the media, publishes game results and league standings (remember that in many recreational programs, it is policy *not* to publish league standings), announces special events or activities (showing soccer films to parents; dates and locations for clinics), publishes articles conducive to the overall promotion of the sport, prepares newsletter for coaches and parents. Other promotional tasks could be assigned to this or a separate committee, such as the sale or distribution of decals, bumper stickers, lapel pins, and so forth.

Age division coordinators. This function has proven very useful for midsize to larger clubs and is appropriate also where the league form of organization has been selected. In a recreational program, the age division coordinator organizes the formation of teams and assists his or her fellow coaches in various ways. It is recommended that the coordinator be elected by the other coaches in the same age division. The coordinator is the focal point for disseminating important information to all coaches. Game scores are phoned in to the coordinator, who is responsible for keeping records or standings and for giving the information to the publicist.

Insignia. The organization should have a logo designed as soon as possible. Each player should be given one or more badges so that one can be affixed to the team jersey and others can be worn on coats, jackets, etc. Lapel pins and the like can also be used for fund-raising.

Insurance. One of the board members should be put in charge of handling the insurance program in accordance with the state association's regulations. Low-cost insurance plans are available for youth soccer for medical and liability coverage. Both are highly recommended. Liability insurance in particular provides protection for all administrators, coaches, referees, and other volunteer workers.

Planning for the Future

Administrators of a newly developed youth soccer organization would be well-advised to keep in contact with their fellow volunteers in well-established leagues or clubs in neighboring areas. An occasional phone call to someone at the state association or at the national level may also prove helpful. In order to better manage the various phases of your program's development, you will benefit from these contacts and the exchanges of information and experiences. Planning ahead will avoid a lot of frustrations later on. The following are a few areas in which planning ahead will prove beneficial.

Advanced Competition

Enjoy the harmony and peace that are typical during the first few years in a new recreational youth soccer program. The times when youngsters are assigned to teams by the coaches involved over a cup of coffee will not last forever. Despite all good intentions, as the program goes on, a small number of coaches may get carried away by their ambitions.

The objective of the league or club administration must be to keep a watchful eye to prevent these happenings, and to carefully monitor the overall development of the organization. It is the administration's responsibility to determine when structured competition and advanced-level teams are to be instituted and to prepare regulations for that phase. Players are entitled to advanced-level competition and formation of select teams or highly competitive teams—when they are technically, physically, and mentally ready; when qualified coaches are available; when regulations for the formation of advanced-level teams are formulated by the league or club; and when a structured league competition can be implemented by taking these teams out of the recreational program.

Teams should not be allowed to operate as more-or-less independent "franchises." It is the organization's responsibility to set up the ground rules for advanced-level play. Contacts with other organizations with experience in this area will assist the newly formed league or club to prepare for this phase of development.

Association Soccer Versus School Soccer

Once a new local program has established itself in the community, the league administrators and parents are likely to develop ambitions of "getting soccer into the schools." After all, participation in a varsity program is still the ultimate recognition for a youngster.

A word of advice is appropriate. Parents must realize that in a developing soccer area, schools are not necessarily in a position to offer good quality coaching. School administrations often require that a varsity coach be a member of the teaching staff. The league or club should try to coordinate with the schools and invite teachers to clinics, or better yet, get them involved in the program. This would be one way of developing soccer coaches who would qualify under school or union regulations *and* would be reasonably well prepared to coach a varsity team. In some cases, the school staff membership requirements have been relaxed, and knowledgeable coaches from the clubs or leagues are permitted to coach varsity teams.

On the other hand, if you are fortunate, you may find qualified soccer coaches in your local schools already. In any case, it helps to establish a good talking or working relationship.

Besides the coaching aspects, you must investigate local high school regulations governing athletic competition. Many state organizations controlling scholastic sports have rules prohibiting youngsters from participating in club soccer while they are playing on the school team. This rule has been successfully challenged in several states. However, it may still be in effect in your area and could present a conflict. Here again, it is useful and will benefit the young players if the league or club establishes contact with the local chapter of the National

Federation of State High School Associations. Such organizations have not always been immediately receptive to requests from soccer organizations, but with patience you should be able to achieve a certain level of understanding and cooperation.

Growth Projections

Evaluation of statistical data can be very useful in many regards. Growth projections are valuable in the overall planning of a local program and particularly in negotiations with city and county agencies on future field requirements. They can also assist in planning uniform purchases, equipment needs, and other aspects of the soccer program.

A new program may find it helpful to look at data from an established organization in a region that is similar in area, population density, and sociological structure. The following examples are based on an actual youth soccer program in a metropolitan area in the Northwest with a population of approximately 2 million.

Figure 1 shows an example of the simplest form of demographics that can be used by a state association as well as at the local level. Plotting on a graph the total player development history (that is, the number of players registered with the program each year) can provide the basis for calculating the program's annual growth rate. This, in turn, will assist in making short-term—and, to some extent, long-term—plans.

Figure 1—Total Player Development History

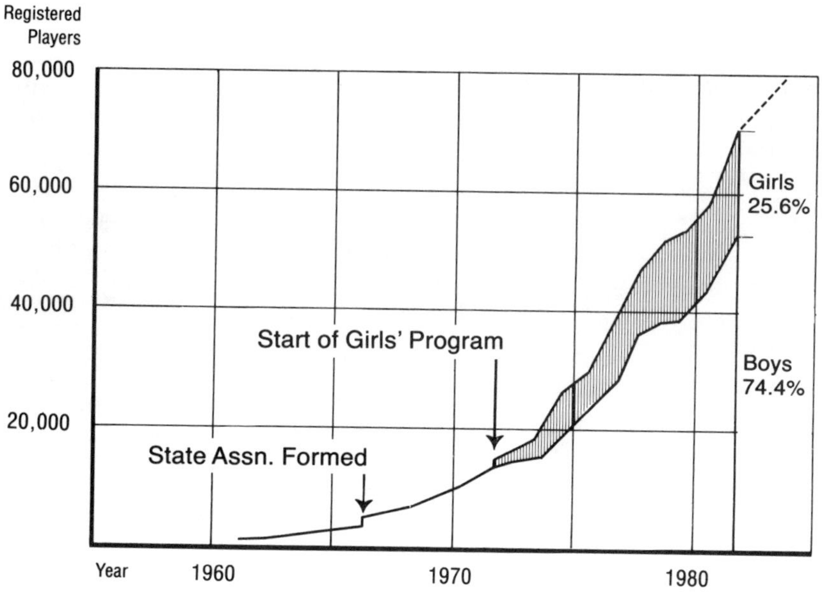

This simple form of demographic analysis is a first step toward establishing growth projections for a soccer program. (Data from an actual program in a metropolitan area of approximately 2 million population.)

Of course, not only may the total number of players change from year to year, the number of players in each age division will also change. (The ages of the participants are important in estimating the number of uniforms to purchase at different sizes, for example.) Figure 2 shows a pattern that is familiar to most experienced administrators. In this instance, the number of players in each age division was plotted for the years 1973 and 1982. Both curves show the drop in participation starting with the teenage years, a phenomenon not restricted to youth soccer and experienced also by associations where soccer has been an established sport for a long time. The explanations for this drop are many, from conflict with jobs to loss of interest because of a lack of continuity in soccer at college or professional levels. A comparison between the curves indicates that, relatively speaking, considerably more older players stayed with the program in 1982 than in 1973, perhaps in part reflecting the remarkable increase in soccer's popularity in recent years. Nonetheless, the pattern of reduced participation by teenagers persists.

Automated Data Processing

An ever-increasing number of households are equipped with a personal

Figure 2—Player Distribution by Age Group

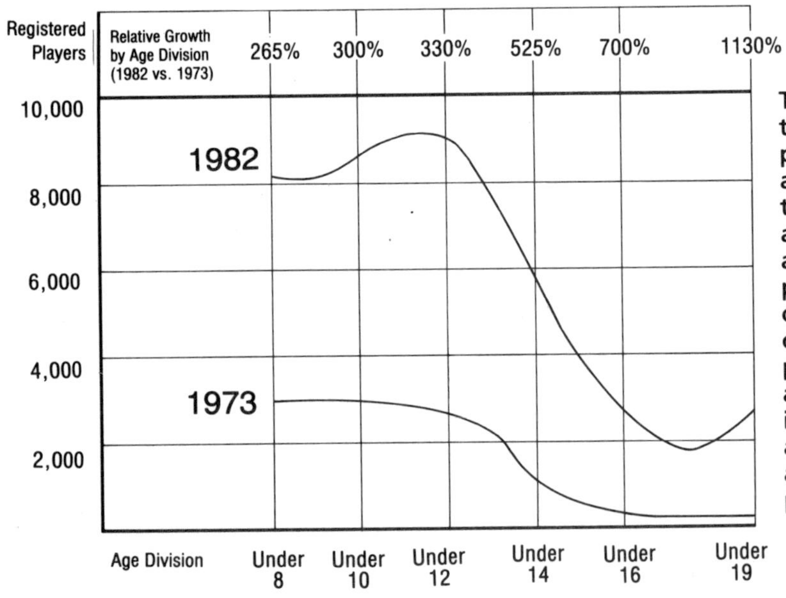

This graph plots the number of participants in each age division for the years 1973 and 1982, and also shows the percentage growth of each age group over the nine-year period. (Data from an actual program in a metropolitan area of approximately 2 million population.)

computer, word processor, or other apparatus for automated data processing. Many of these devices can be employed in running the day-to-day business of a local youth soccer organization. Automated data processing can make many tasks manageable for the average volunteer: player and team registration, including updates in case of additions or transfers; directories for administrators, coaches, referees; mailing labels for selected groups or for entire organizations; records of scores and maintenance of league standings; game schedules and field assignments; bookkeeping.

Many local and state associations are using automated data processing. A new organization should check with its state youth association about the availability of such a service.

The preceding discussion is only a general outline of what is involved in starting and running a youth soccer program. The actual approach will vary depending on local circumstances. If the organizers entrusted with the task of setting up the program display good leadership qualities, are able to inspire others, and are devoted to the recreational aspects of youth soccer, the organization is bound to enjoy great success.

Appendix

Laws of the Game Summarized, with Modifications for Youth Soccer

The rules of soccer, or Laws of the Game, as they are officially called, are controlled by FIFA. Changes in the rules can be made only with the approval of USYSA/USSF and FIFA. The summary below is a condensed version of the 17 Laws of the Game and should provide a good introduction to the finer points of the soccer rules.

The person who wants to become actively involved in soccer as a coach or referee or even as an occasional linesman should obtain a copy of the complete Laws of the Game (available from the USYSA). The official rule book contains such useful information as interpretations of the rules made by the International Board, detailed explanations of the offside rule, special instructions to referees and linesmen, regulations covering the taking of penalty kicks as a tie-breaker, and signals for referees and linesmen.

Study of the rules and official interpretations indicates that once the fundamentals of the game are understood, common sense can be the basis for applying the Laws of the Game and making additional interpretations. Unofficially, soccer people often refer to Law 18—Use common sense!

For example, in youth soccer it would make sense, if the referee for some reason does not show up for a game, for the two coaches to select another referee from the persons present instead of not playing the match. Common sense also tells us that one of the major objectives of the laws of soccer is to protect players from injury. Therefore, anything that could potentially present a danger, even if it is not specifically covered in the rules, should be avoided.

Approved modifications to the Laws of the Game for youth soccer are stated in Section 21 of the USYSA bylaws and in policies published from time to time by the USYSA. These modifications have been incorporated in the following summary and are printed in **boldface** type. They pertain to Law 1–Field of Play; Law 2–The Ball; Law 3–Number of Players (and Substitutions); Law 4–Players' Equipment; and Law 7–Duration of the Game. Additional adjustments to the Laws of the Game for *local* play or young player development programs are permitted, as long as they do not alter the spirit of the FIFA laws.

Law 1 – Field of Play

1. A proper field of play is rectangular and consists of an outer boundary, two goals at opposite ends of the field, a penalty area, a halfway line, and a few other more specialized markings. Corner flags and clear markings are necessary to assist the players and the referee during the conduct of the game. The outer boundary lines are part of the field of play. (The drawing of the field in Chapter 1 shows the proper markings.)
2. FIFA rules provide that the field must be between 50 and 100 yards wide and between 100 and 130 yards long, although FIFA designates the preferred dimensions as between 70 and 80 yards wide and between 110 and 120 yards long.

   For players under 12 smaller fields are recommended. The size will vary with age and the number of players on a team, depending on the guidelines used locally for the player development program. Recommended dimensions are width approximately 35 to 50 yards and length approximately 70 to 90 yards.
3. Regulation goals are eight yards wide and eight feet high (inside dimensions).

   For players under 12 smaller goals are recommended. The scale-down factor is left to the discretion of the local organization. The following may be used as a general guideline: Seven yards by seven feet for Under 12; six yards by six feet for Under 8; five yards by five feet for age 6 and under.
4. The penalty area is a rectangular area in front of each goal with lines 18 yards in front of the goal and from each goalpost.

   Smaller penalty areas are recommended for players under 12, using the same scale factor as for the goal size.
5. The goal area is a rectangular area in front of each goal with lines six yards in front of the goal and from each goalpost.

   When field dimensions are scaled down for younger age divisions, the goal area may also be scaled down as described above.

6. The corner area is a quarter circle at each corner of the field having a radius of one yard.

Law 2 – The Ball

1. The size and weight of the ball shall comply with the following specifications (size #5 corresponds to FIFA regulations, other sizes are modifications for youth soccer):

AGE DIVISION	SIZE	CIRCUMFERENCE	WEIGHT
Under 19, 16, 14	**#5**	**27–28 in.**	**14–16 oz.**
Under 12, 10	**#4**	**25–26 in.**	**11–13 oz.**
Under 8	**#3**	**23–24 in.**	**11–12 oz.**

   The ball (#5) should be inflated to between 9.0 and 10.5 pounds per square inch at sea level. Use less pressure for higher altitudes and for the smaller sizes (follow manufacturer's specifications).
2. The material and construction of the ball must not be dangerous for the players.

Law 3 – Number of Players (and Substitutions)

1. A full team on the field consists of 11 players, one of whom shall be the goalkeeper. Both FIFA and the USYSA/USSF recommend that a game not be considered valid if there are fewer than seven players on the field for either of the teams.

   For children 10 years of age or younger, the USYSA recommends mini-soccer games with a reduced number of players on a side; for example, nine players for teams of 9- and 10-year-olds, seven players for teams of 8-year-olds.
2. Any of the field players may change places with the goalkeeper, with the consent of the referee, provided the change is made during a stoppage of the game.
3. An ejected player may not be replaced.
4. The number of substitutions is limited to two per game. A player who has been replaced shall not return to the game.

   For youth competitions under the auspices of the USYSA, substitutions shall be unlimited. A player who has been replaced may return to the game. Substitutions may be made, with the consent of the referee, at the following times:
   - **Prior to a throw-in in favor of team substituting**
   - **Prior to a goal kick (by either team)**
   - **After a goal (by either team)**
   - **After an injury (either team) when the referee stops play**
   - **At halftime**

Law 4 – Players' Equipment

1. A player shall not wear anything that is dangerous to another player (for example, a watch, certain rings, an unpadded wrist cast).

2. Shoes must comply with detailed safety standards. Molded plastic soles with studs must have at least ten studs, which must be at least 3/8 inch in diameter and not more than 3/4 inch in height. Replaceable studs must be round and not more than 1/2 inch in diameter and not more than 3/4 inch in height and must be made of a safe material and construction (the screw must be part of the cleat, not embedded in the sole).

   Depending on the playing facilities, the local organization may issue regulations regarding the type of shoes that may be used for youth soccer. Sneakers may be worn by players.
3. Uniforms consist of shorts, shirts, and knee socks.

   Numbers on the back of the shirts are optional for youth play but may be required for certain competitions. They shall be at least eight inches high and easily discernible from the sidelines.
4. The goalkeeper shall wear a different color shirt than the referee and the other players (both teams).

Law 5 – Referees

1. The referee has jurisdiction from the time he enters the field of play until he signals the end of the game. His decisions are final.
2. The referee shall enforce the Laws of the Game but shall refrain from stopping the game for an infraction when he is satisfied that by doing so he would be giving an advantage to the offending team.
3. The referee can stop the game for infringement of the rules (by blowing a whistle).
4. The referee can suspend or terminate a game whenever he deems necessary (for example, because of severe weather or interference by spectators or coaches).
5. The referee can caution a player and shall eject from play any player guilty of violent conduct or serious foul play, use of foul or abusive language, or persistent infringement of the playing rules.
6. The referee acts as the timekeeper and keeps a record of the game.

Law 6 – Linesmen

1. Two linesmen shall be appointed to assist the referee.
2. The duties of the linesmen are to signal by use of the linesman's flag
   - When the ball is out of play
   - Which team is entitled to the corner kick, goal kick, or throw-in
   - When an offside infraction has occurred
   - When an infraction has occurred that the referee may not have seen
3. The referee always makes the final decision of the action to be taken even if the initial linesman's signal is to the contrary. Only the referee can stop the game.

Law 7 – Duration of the Game

1. The duration of the game shall be two equal periods of 45 minutes. Overtime periods (two 15-minute halves) are used in certain cup and tournament competitions if the game is tied at the end of regulation time. If the game is still tied after overtime periods, FIFA tie-breaking rules involving kicks from the penalty mark will apply in order to determine a winner.

   The following time periods apply to youth soccer:

AGE DIVISION	GAME LENGTH	OVERTIME PERIODS
Under 19	**Two 45-minute halves**	**Two 15-minute halves**
Under 16	**Two 40-minute halves**	**Two 15-minute halves**
Under 14	**Two 35-minute halves**	**Two 10-minute halves**
Under 12	**Two 30-minute halves**	**Two 10-minute halves**
Under 10	**Two 25-minute halves**	**Two 10-minute halves**
Under 8	**Two 25-minute halves**	**Two 5-minute halves**

   Additional adjustments to playing times may be made by the local association for players under 12 in mini-soccer or mod soccer development programs.
2. Allowance shall be made by the referee for time lost through injuries or other causes.
3. Players have a right to a five-minute break at halftime.

Law 8 – Start of Play

1. The start of play at the beginning of each half and after a goal shall proceed with a kickoff.
2. At the beginning of the game, the choice of the ends or kickoff shall be determined by the toss of a coin. The team winning the toss shall have the option of the choice of ends or kickoff.
3. After halftime, the ends shall be changed and the kickoff shall be taken by the team opposite from the team that took the kickoff at the beginning of the game.
4. On a kickoff, the ball must be stationary on the ground at the center of the field and must travel the distance of its circumference into the opponent's half of the field before being in play. If this rule is violated, the kickoff shall be retaken.
5. The player taking the kickoff may not play the ball a second time until it has been touched by another player. If this rule is violated, the opposing team is awarded an indirect free kick.
6. Every player on each team must be in his own half of the field, and all players of the team opposing the kicker must be at least ten yards away from the ball when the ball is put into play. If this rule is violated, the kickoff shall be retaken.
7. A goal cannot be scored directly from a kickoff.
8. After a temporary suspension of play for any reason not otherwise mentioned in the Laws of the Game, the referee shall restart the game by a drop ball where the ball was when play was stopped. A

player may not play the ball until it touches the ground. If this rule is violated, the drop ball shall be retaken. A goal may be scored directly from a drop ball.

Law 9 – Ball In and Out of Play

1. The ball is out of play only
   - When it has crossed the goal line or touchline in its entirety, whether on the ground or in the air
   - When the game has been stopped by the referee
2. The ball is in play at all other times during the game, even if
   - It rebounds from a goalpost, crossbar, or corner flag into the field of play
   - It rebounds off the referee or a linesman when he is in the field of play
   - An apparent infraction has occurred but the referee has not stopped the game

Law 10 – Method of Scoring

1. A goal is scored when the whole of the ball crosses the goal line between the goalposts and under the crossbar, provided it was not thrown, carried, or intentionally propelled by arm or hand by an attacking player (except the opposing goalkeeper who throws the ball from his own penalty area).
2. If a defending player deflects the ball with his hand or arm and the ball goes in the goal, a goal is scored ("own goal").
3. The team scoring more goals during the game wins.
4. The game results in a "tie" if no team scores or if each team scores an equal number of goals.
5. In cup or tournament play, if a game is still tied after overtime periods, FIFA tie-breaking rules involving kicks from the penalty mark will apply (see Law 7).

Law 11 – Offside

1. A player is in an offside position if he is nearer the opposing team's goal line than the ball at the moment the ball is played unless
   - He is in his own half of the field
   - Two opposing players are nearer their goal line than he is (including the opposing goalkeeper)
   - The ball is last touched by an opponent
   - He received the ball directly from a goal kick, corner kick, throw-in, or drop ball
2. A player in an offside position is not offside unless, in the opinion of the referee, he is seeking to gain advantage by being in an offside position.
3. For an offside infraction, the defending team is awarded an indirect free kick from the place where the offside occurred.

Law 12 – Fouls and Misconduct

1. Fouls and misconduct are penalized by awarding free kicks to the opposing team. The guilty player may also be cautioned or ejected, even if a free kick is not awarded due to application of the advantage clause (Law 5).
2. The following nine fouls are penalized by awarding a direct free kick to the opposing team:
   - Intentionally kicking or attempting to kick an opponent
   - Intentionally tripping or attempting to trip an opponent
   - Intentionally jumping at an opponent
   - Intentionally charging an opponent violently
   - Intentionally charging an opponent from behind
   - Intentionally striking or attempting to strike an opponent
   - Intentionally holding an opponent
   - Intentionally pushing an opponent
   - Intentionally handling the ball (except as a goalkeeper inside the penalty area)

   A direct free kick offense committed in the guilty player's penalty area is a penalty kick.
3. The following five rule infractions are penalized by awarding an indirect free kick to the opposing team:
   - Dangerous play
   - Charging fairly when not in playing distance of the ball
   - Obstructing an opponent
   - Charging the goalkeeper inside his goal area
   - A goalkeeper who is playing within his own penalty area and (a) delays the game, *or* (b) after saving and controlling the ball, takes more than four steps without releasing it, *or* (c) after having released the ball, plays it again before another player has touched it
4. A player shall be cautioned (referee shows yellow card) if he
   - Persistently infringes the Laws of the Game
   - Dissents from any decision of the referee
   - Is guilty of ungentlemanly conduct
   - Enters or reenters the field without the referee's permission
5. A player shall be ejected from the game (referee shows red card) if he
   - Is guilty of violent conduct or serious foul play
   - Uses foul or abusive language
   - Persists in misconduct after having received a caution (yellow card)

   An ejected player may not be replaced.

Law 13 – Free Kicks

1. The two kinds of free kicks are
   - Direct free kicks (from which a goal may be scored direct against the offending team)

- Indirect free kicks (from which a goal cannot be scored unless the ball is touched by a player other than the kicker before going into the goal)

2. Direct free kicks are awarded only for the nine direct free kick fouls under Law 12. All other offenses are awarded an indirect free kick unless specifically stated otherwise in the law that describes the offense.
3. A free kick is taken from the place where the offense occurred.
4. The ball must be stationary on the ground, must travel the distance of its circumference before being in play, and may not be played by the kicker a second time before being touched by another player.
5. All opposing players must be at least ten yards away from the ball when the ball is put into play. If this rule is violated, the free kick is retaken.
6. If the offense occurred less than ten yards from the opponents' goal line, the opposing players may stand on their own goal line between the goalposts.
7. On free kicks taken within its penalty area by the defending team, all opposing players must be outside the penalty area and at least ten yards away from the ball. The ball must travel outside the penalty area before being in play.

Law 14 – Penalty Kick

1. A penalty kick is awarded if the defending team commits one of the nine direct free kick fouls within its own penalty area.
2. The penalty kick is taken from the penalty mark, which is centered 12 yards in front of the goal.
3. All players except the kicker and the goalkeeper must be outside the penalty area and at least ten yards away from the penalty mark.
4. The goalkeeper must stand with both feet touching the goal line and must not move his feet until the ball is kicked.
5. The ball must be kicked forward, must travel the distance of its circumference before being in play, and may not be played by the kicker a second time before being touched by another player.
6. A goal may be scored directly on a penalty kick.
7. For any violation of this law
   - If by the kicker, an indirect free kick is awarded the defending team
   - If by the attacking team other than the kicker and a goal results, the penalty kick shall be retaken
   - If by the defending team and a goal does not result, the penalty kick shall be retaken
8. Time shall be extended to allow a penalty kick to be taken.

Law 15 – Throw-in

1. A throw-in is awarded if the ball passes completely over a touchline, either on the ground or in the air.

2. The ball is thrown in at the place where it crossed the line by a player of the team opposite to that of the player who last touched it.
3. The thrower must face the field and part of each foot must be on the ground, either on the touchline or outside the field of play. The ball must be thrown with both hands and must be delivered from behind and over his head.
4. A goal cannot be scored directly from a throw-in.
5. If the throw-in is improper, a throw-in from the same place shall be awarded to the opposing team.
6. The ball is in play immediately upon entering the field of play, but may not be played by the thrower before being touched by another player.

Law 16 – Goal Kick

1. A goal kick is awarded the defending team if the ball passes completely over its goal line, outside the goal, after having last been touched by a player of the attacking team.
2. The goal kick is taken from any point within that half of the goal area nearest the place where the ball crossed the goal line.
3. All opposing players must be outside the penalty area.
4. The ball must travel outside the penalty area before being in play and may not be played by the kicker a second time before being touched by another player.
5. A goal cannot be scored directly from a goal kick.
6. If the ball does not travel outside the penalty area, the goal kick shall be retaken.

Law 17 – Corner Kick

1. A corner kick is awarded the attacking team if the ball passes completely over the defending team's goal line, outside the goal, after having last been touched by a player of the defending team.
2. The corner kick is taken from within the quarter circle nearest the place where the ball crossed the goal line.
3. All opposing players must be at least ten yards away from the ball.
4. The ball must travel the distance of its circumference before being in play, and may not be played by the kicker a second time before being touched by another player.
5. A goal may be scored directly from a corner kick.
6. If the kicker plays the ball before it is touched by another player, the opposing team shall be awarded an indirect free kick. For any other violation of this law, the corner kick shall be retaken.

Glossary of Soccer Terms

Advantage Clause: A provision in the Laws of the Game that allows the referee to let play continue in the case of a rule infraction when, in his judgment, awarding the penalty would be of advantage to the offending team. The referee must signal "play on."

Backs: See Fullbacks.

Ball Control: General term for the various techniques of bringing a moving ball under control. See also Collecting.

Ball Pendulum: A training aid featuring a ball suspended on a cord.

Block Tackle: Attempting to take the ball from an opponent by blocking it with the inside of the foot at the same time that he is attempting to kick it in the opposite direction.

Catching: A specific goalkeeper skill used in collecting or saving shots with the hands. The goalkeeper is the only player allowed to catch the ball and may do so only within the penalty area.

Caution: A disciplinary action taken by the referee against a player guilty of misconduct, signaled by showing a yellow card. The referee must verbally warn the player and record the action. A second offense by the same player results in ejection (red card). Cautions can also be issued to players on the bench and to coaches.

Center Circle: The circle at the center of the field, which defines the distance of opposing players from the ball at the kickoff. Drawn with a ten-yard radius on a full-size field, the center circle may be drawn with a smaller radius on a scaled-down field for young players.

Center Forward: A forward operating in the center of the attack. It is the key position in the classic offense-oriented team formations. Also called "central striker."

Centering: Passing the ball from the side of the field to a player or open space in front of the goal. See also Cross Pass.

Center Spot: The midpoint of the center circle, from which kickoffs are taken.

Charging: Making shoulder-to-shoulder contact with an opponent in an attempt to set him off-balance and gain control of the ball (no elbow or arm action is allowed). The shoulder-to-shoulder charge is the only deliberate body contact permitted in game action and is allowable only when the ball is within playing distance.

Chip Pass: A pass made on a steep trajectory, often used to lob the ball over a wall of defenders.

Clearing: Passing, kicking, heading, or throwing the ball (throwing by the goalkeeper only) to move it away from one's own goal area.

Collecting: Any technique of receiving a moving ball in the air or on the ground and controlling it before passing or shooting.

Combination Play: A series of passes made between two or more players with emphasis on maintaining possession of the ball and controlled build-up of an attack.

Corner Area: A quarter-circle arc (radius one yard) drawn at each corner of the field, from which corner kicks are taken.

Corner Flag: The flag positioned at each of the four corners of the field. Flagsticks are five feet high. They must not be removed when corner kicks are taken.

Corner Kick: A placekick taken by an attacking player from the corner area after the ball has gone out-of-bounds across the goal line and was last touched by a defender.

Covering: Staying close to an attacking opponent, usually goal-side, ready to challenge him when he is receiving the ball.

Cross Pass: A pass from one side of the field to the other or to the area in front of the goal mouth, usually to set up a teammate for a shot on goal. See also Centering.

Dangerous Play: Playing in a manner that could cause injury to another player if contact were to be made. Penalty: Indirect free kick.

Dead-Ball Situation: Any time the ball is played from a static position, such as a kickoff, corner kick, goal kick, free kick, or throw-in.

Direct Free Kick: A free kick from which a goal can be scored directly, that is, without the ball having to be touched first by a player other than the kicker. See also Indirect Free Kick.

Diving: A method used by the goalkeeper to deflect shots on goal.

Dribbling: Propelling and controlling the ball with a series of short, soft touches with the foot, usually making changes in pace and direction, without passing to a teammate.

Drop Ball: A ball dropped by the referee between two opposing players to restart the game after play has been stopped for reasons *other than* rule infractions, ball out of play, or a goal having been scored (for example, because of an injured player). The ball can be played only after it has dropped on the ground. The drop ball takes place at the location of the ball at the moment the game was stopped.

Ejection: Sending a player off the field for repeated rule violations after having been cautioned, or for use of foul or abusive language, violent conduct, or serious foul play. An ejected player (signaled by the referee with a red card) cannot be replaced.

Feinting: Using deceptive body moves to put an opponent off-guard in one-on-one situations.

FIFA: Fédération Internationale de Football Association (International Federation of Association Football), the world governing body of soccer with more than 150 national associations, headquartered in Zurich, Switzerland. FIFA has control over the Laws of the Game and international competition.

Forwards: Players with predominantly offensive tasks, particularly scoring goals. Also called "strikers."

Free Kick: A placekick awarded after a rule infraction by the other team. Opposing players must remain ten or more yards from the ball until it is put in play. See also Direct Free Kick; Indirect Free Kick.

Fullbacks: Defenders forming the last group of players in front of the goal. Predominantly defense-oriented, they must quickly initiate an attack after gaining possession of the ball. Also called "backs."

Goal: (1) The area at each end of the field into which the ball must be propelled in order to score. On a full-size field, goalposts are eight yards apart and the crossbar is eight feet high; goal dimensions may be reduced on a scaled-down field for young players. (2) The term for a score, which results from propelling the whole of the ball completely behind the outer boundary of the goal line between the goalposts and below the crossbar. Each goal scored counts one point.

Goal Area: The small rectangular area (six yards deep and 20 yards wide on full-size fields) in front of the goal. Goal kicks are taken from within this area. The goalkeeper cannot be charged in the goal area.

Goalkeeper: A special defender with the task of saving shots on goal. The goalkeeper is the only player who can play the ball with his hands, but not outside the penalty area.

Goal Kick: A placekick taken from within the goal area by a member of the defending team when the ball goes out-of-bounds across the goal line and was last touched by a member of the attacking team. The ball is in play after it travels outside the penalty area, and opposing players may not enter the penalty area until this happens.

Goal Line: The boundary line at each end of the field. When the ball crosses this line between the goalposts and under the crossbar, a goal is scored. When the ball crosses the goal line outside the goalposts, play is restarted by a corner kick or a goal kick.

Halfbacks: See Midfielders.

Half-Volley Kick: A kick taken just after the ball bounces off the ground.

Hand Ball: A violation of the rule stating that the ball must not be played with the hands or the arms below the shoulder by players other than the goalkeeper. Penalty: Direct free kick or penalty kick.

Heading: The technique of propelling the ball with the forehead.

Holding: Intentionally using the hands or arms to impede an opposing player's movements; an offense penalized by a direct free kick.

Indirect Free Kick: A free kick from which a goal cannot be scored directly; the ball must first be touched or played by a player other than the kicker.

Indoor Soccer: The term for variations of soccer played indoors, usually as small-sided games and usually during winter.

Inside Forwards: In the classic team formations, the forwards playing inside the wingers and on either side of the center forward.

Juggling: Keeping the ball in the air by using various parts of the body except the hands and arms. An exercise for developing ball control.

Kickoff: A placekick taken from the center spot to start the game or to restart it after a goal has been scored or after halftime.

Laws of the Game: Formal name for the rules of soccer, which are controlled by FIFA.

Libero: See Sweeper.

Linesmen: The two officials who assist the referee. They move along the touchlines on opposite sides of the field, each covering one half of the field, and signal the referee with flags for a ball out-of-bounds, an offside, or an infraction the referee may not have seen. The referee can overrule the linesmen.

Linkmen: See Midfielders.

Lob Pass: See Chip Pass.

Man-to-Man Defense: A defensive tactic requiring defenders to mark or guard specific attacking players. See also Covering; Zone Defense.

Marking: Guarding or covering an opponent.

Midfielders: Players who function primarily between fullbacks and forwards to build up an attack or help in defense. Also called "halfbacks" or "linkmen."

Obstruction: When ball is *not* within playing distance, preventing or trying to prevent an opponent from reaching the ball or getting into position to receive a pass. A violation penalized by an indirect free kick.

Off-the-Ball Play: A tactic whereby players not in ball possession move around to be in good position to receive a pass or draw an opposing player away to create an opening.

Offside: A player is in an offside position if he is between his opponent's goal line and the ball at the moment the ball is played unless (1) he is in his own half of the field, (2) at least two opponents (including the goalkeeper) are nearer their own goal line than he is, or (3) he received the ball directly from a corner kick, goal kick, throw-in, or drop-ball situation or from an opposing player. A violation is penalized by an indirect free kick.

One-Touch: Passing or shooting on goal without first stopping the ball, i.e., with one touch.

Open Space: Area on the field of play not being covered by opposing players. "Using the open spaces" means passing the ball into an open area where a teammate can run to it and safely collect it. "Creating an open space" means running when not in possession of the ball to a different position and drawing an opponent to that new position. Also called "opening."

Out of Play: The ball is out of play when (1) it has completely crossed the outer edges of the touchlines or goal lines, or (2) the referee has stopped play.

Outside Forwards: Forwards operating primarily near the touchlines, who typically penetrate deep into the opponent's half of the field and center the ball in front of the goal. Also called "wingers."

Own Goal: A goal accidentally scored for the opposition by a player of the defending team, usually the result of a deflection of a hard shot.

Passing: Propelling the ball by kicking or heading it to a teammate or an open space where it can be safely collected by a teammate.

Passing Combination: General term for specific combinations of passes or types of passes, such as the wall pass.

Penalty Area: The large rectangular area (18 by 44 yards on full-size fields) in front of the goal. The goalkeeper can play the ball with his hands only within this area. Direct free kick offenses committed by a defender inside this area are awarded a penalty kick.

Penalty Kick: A direct free kick taken from the penalty mark. All players, with the exception of the goalkeeper and the player taking the kick, must be outside the penalty area and ten yards from the ball. The goalkeeper must have part of both feet on the goal line until the ball is in play.

Penalty Mark: The place in front of the center of the goal line from which penalty kicks are taken (located 12 yards from the goal on full-size fields).

Pitch: The traditional name for a soccer field (British terminology).

Placekick: A kick taken when the ball has been placed in a stationary position, as for a kickoff or free kick.

Play On: Call and/or signal by the referee when he applies the advantage clause.

Punching: Deflection of the ball by goalkeeper with one or both fists.

Push Pass: A short pass executed with the inner side of the foot.

Reading the Game: The ability of a player to analyze the opposing team's moves, thereby developing an understanding of their tactics and their standard passing combinations.

Referee: The official in charge of enforcing the Laws of the Game during a soccer match. The referee is the sole judge and timekeeper and keeps records of the score and player cautions or ejections. He is assisted by two linesmen.

Restart: The term for recommencing play after dead-ball situations, including drop balls, free kicks, and throw-ins.

Save: A successful effort by the goalkeeper to prevent a possible score by stopping or deflecting a ball aimed at the goal.

Screening: Staying between an opposing player and the ball when dribbling in order to shield it and prevent the opponent from playing it. Also called "shielding."

Shooting: Kicking the ball on goal with the intent of scoring.

Sidelines: See Touchlines.

Sliding Tackle: A tackle whereby the player slides on the ground, supporting himself on the calf and thigh of one leg, and pushes the ball away from the opponent with the other foot.

Square Pass: A pass made laterally.

Stopper: A central defender who usually marks the opposing center forward. Also called "center fullback."

Strikers: See Forwards.

Support: Backing up a teammate with the ball in order to receive a pass or tackle an opposing player who might gain possession.

Sweeper: In a group of defenders, the player whose task it is to intercept an opposing forward who has beaten the defender assigned to cover him. Also called "libero."

System of Play: See Team Formation.

Tackling: Trying to take possession of the ball from an opposing player by using the feet, as in passing or kicking. Tackling must always be directed at the ball; body impact with the other player is not allowed. See also Block Tackle; Sliding Tackle.

Team Formation: The arrangement of the ten field players in functional positions. Usually a numerical description is given, such as 4-3-3 or 4-2-4, referring to the number of designated defenders (first number), midfield players, and forwards. Also called "system of play."

Throw-In: The method of putting the ball in play after it has gone out-of-bounds over a touchline. The ball is thrown in at the same location it went out by a player opposite the team that last touched it. The thrower must have a part of both feet on the ground, either on or behind the touchline, must face the field of play, and must throw the ball equally with both hands from behind the head. A goal cannot be scored directly from a throw-in.

Time Outs: There are none in soccer. It is left to the discretion of the referee to stop play when a player is injured.

Touchlines: The boundary lines at each side of the field. Also called "sidelines."

USSF: United States Soccer Federation—the national governing body for soccer in the United States, with three divisions: senior amateur, youth, and professional. It receives its charter from FIFA and the U.S. Olympic Committee.

USYSA: United States Youth Soccer Association—the youth division of the USSF, responsible for soccer for players under 19 years of age. The USYSA comprises state youth soccer associations.

Volley Kick: A kick taken before the ball touches the ground.

Wall Pass: A basic passing combination whereby a player makes a short diagonal pass to a teammate who serves as a "wall" to deflect the ball forward. The first player sprints ahead to collect the ball.

Wingers: See Outside Forwards.

World Cup: The world championship of soccer, conducted under the auspices of FIFA. The competition is open to teams formed from the best players of a country (national teams), amateur or professional. Preliminary playoffs in six continental federations determine the participants in the final playoff rounds (usually 16 or 24 teams). The World Cup is played every four years and is the world's largest international sports event in attendance and television audience.

Zone Defense: A defensive tactical concept in which each defender is assigned the task of covering a particular area (zone) of the field. See also Man-to-Man Defense.